# The Pandemic Prophet

*A Soulistic View of the Socioeconomic Guinea Worms of Modern Minds*

## The Legacy of Reginald E. Petty
## As told to Jaye P. Willis

Copyright © 2022 by Jaye P. Willis.

ISBN 978-1-958678-47-3 (softcover)
ISBN 978-1-958678-48-0 (hardcover)
ISBN 978-1-958678-49-7 (ebook)
Library of Congress Control Number: 2022914961

All rights reserved. No part of this book may be reproduced or transmitted in any form or by any means, electronic or mechanical, including photocopying, recording, or by any information storage and retrieval system without express written permission from the author, except in the case of brief quotations embodied in critical reviews and certain other noncommercial uses permitted by copyright law.

Printed in the United States of America.

Book Vine Press
2516 Highland Dr.
Palatine, IL 60067

# DEDICATION

This book is dedicated to the young people existing in despair and reaching out for hope. My greatest desire is that this book take them to a place of joy where they will begin to challenge their conditions and set goals for a life where their gifts can be realized and shared.

I also dedicate this book to my father, Jerome Harris, whose daily inspiration and acceptance of my whole being gave me the courage to pursue my dream of writing.

To my mother, husband, and children. I thank you for your patience and support during this time of extreme turmoil and joy in my life.

To Reg and Edna, and the Petty clan, thank you, for allowing me to share your story.

I love you all.

# ABOUT THE TITLE

As this book is being published in the midst of the coronavirus pandemic (aka Covid-19), the irony of the title chosen for this biography over five years ago is not lost on me. The current state of the world, especially the United States of America, can still benefit from the trials and tribulations of this amazing man, Reginald E. Petty, whose life experiences predicted and epitomize our current state.

The title may be long but has significant meaning that I want to share with the reader. Mr. Petty found *The Pandemic Prophet: A Soulistic View of the Socioeconomic Guinea Worms of Modern Minds* both inventive and acceptable. Members of my family and friends found it too long and in need of major explaining before they would even venture to read the book. When I mentioned this to Mr. Petty, he reminded me that I am the author. I am empowered and do not need anyone else's acceptance of my vision. I love this dude so much!

The pandemic is not of the body but the mind. The word 'soulistic' is a neologism used to express the deep core of our being that drives us to be human. Guinea worms are parasites that live in unpurified drinking water. They enter the body when unclean drinking water is ingested. They thrive on the fluids in the host body until growing to size or maturing and then exiting the body through the skin. It is my contention that beliefs like racism, bigotry, intolerance, and all manner of evil against our fellow man are Guinea worms that enter our bodies via unfiltered thoughts. The worms then manifest themselves or leave our minds via opinions that lead to unjust legislation or policies or misconceptions that adversely affect a core group of people. Reg points to many of these modern mind Guinea worms through his interactions with people all over the world. It is an honor to place these thoughts into written form to share with all people and hopefully, make this world a better place.

# CONTENTS

Dedication .................................................................................. iii

About the Title ............................................................................ v

Prologue .................................................................................... ix

Reflections by J.A. Brown............................................................ 1

Introduction by Reginald Petty..................................................... 5

One Score: Conceived Through Segregation ................................ 7

Two Score: Transplanting Knowledge ......................................... 21

Three Score: Swaziland to Swagger-land .................................... 49

Four Score: Pandemic Parle ........................................................ 89

Five Score: Eternal Vigil ............................................................. 97

Epilogue ................................................................................... 115

About the Author ..................................................................... 119

Index ........................................................................................ 121

# PROLOGUE

It always amazes me how people view the landmarks right in front of them. Living less than six miles from St. Louis, Missouri all my life, I would not enter the famous St. Louis Gateway Arch until I was 22 years of age. People from all over the world had visited the Arch, taken the tram to the top and looked out over the Mississippi riverfront, viewing East St. Louis, Illinois and St. Louis, Missouri.

I guess it is because we live (work, play, attend school) in these locations that the fascination these landmarks provide to strangers does not really attract the locals. But this sense of apathy towards local marvels does not just extend itself to buildings but to people as well, people who have made a difference in their community, state, region, country, and the world. People who have represented the city of their rearing to the masses with great pride and distinction, yet live in anonymity to the very people in need of the light these people possess; a light that can lead the way to a great healing of despair – HOPE. Reginald Edwin Petty is such a man.

As I was a late bloomer in partaking of the marvels of the St. Louis Arch, I was an even later bloomer in partaking of the beauty and wisdom, knowledge, gentle nature and passion of Mr. Petty, affectionately known as Reg. His life is one of intrigue, civil disobedience, moral fortitude, accomplishment and travel, most of which has not even been a dream of some residents of the Southern counties of Illinois. It is my greatest hope that the words from this book via the mouth of this great man, reach the sleeping minds of the youth of East St. Louis and all cities like it worldwide, and 'wake them up' to the possibilities of what can be, of what another poor youth from their hometown attained through education, hard work, confidence, a loving foundation and courage.

Reg holds the normal banners of most men. He is a son, brother, husband, father, grandfather, uncle, and cousin. In addition to these, though, is where his distinctions abound. Reg has received presidential appointments from Presidents John F. Kennedy, Lyndon B. Johnson, Gerald Ford, and Jimmy Carter. He was one of the first African American Peace Corps Country Directors (Burkina Faso) and established one of the first Job Corps Centers in Breckenridge, Kentucky. He speaks fluent French, met with and talked politics with world leaders such as Nelson Mandela and addressed civil rights issues with activists Stokely Carmichael, John Lewis, and Dr. Martin Luther King, Jr. He was a good friend and confidante of the one and only Malcolm X. These and additional fascinating accomplishments of this man will be discussed in the following pages.

It is amazing to me that I, as a young student growing up in East St. Louis, was not made aware of the existence or accomplishments of Reginald Petty. In a city full of black pride, where schools are named after famous Afro people of local and national fame, including Crispus Attucks…and public housing such as Attorney Louie Orr and Dr. Henry Weathers… It dumbfounds me that there is not an annual celebration of Reginald Petty, a street named after him, a school named after him, a commemorative day set aside to honor him. I wonder why his accomplishments are not required reading in the city schools and the teachers mandated to know who he is and be tested on their knowledge of outstanding people and events in East St. Louis, Illinois, now known as the City of Champions.

In this small area or per capita of Illinois, the proportion of greatness from this city is staggering. From a U.S. Ambassador to internationally renowned Jazz musicians; an international president of Sigma Gamma Rho Sorority, Incorporated; three U.S. Olympic Champions; a national president of Jack and Jill of America, Incorporated; a national president of Top Ladies of Distinction, Incorporated; Super Bowl winners; state champion football and basketball teams; one of the first Poet Laureates of a city within the United States, and many, many other accomplishments too numerous to mention. How has the greatness of this man sat in the shadows and not been recognized for the inspiration that his life provides?

It is the intention of this book to shed light on the storied career of Reginald Edwin Petty, including his observations over the past 80 plus years, both from a national and international perspective, his witticisms, and his advice for a better future for the students of East St. Louis, Illinois, and the world. He has made a significant impact on my life and the lives of my immediate family. As they take this journey of discovery of the man, Reg Petty, they learn something new about themselves and life in general. It is commonplace to sit in his home where he receives phone calls from esteemed educator Dr. Harry Edwards or former United States Ambassador to the United Nations Donald McHenry.

The format of this book allows for Black History education as well. Many of the people that Reg encountered have made an indelible imprint on American and World history themselves. A brief synopsis of their accomplishments follows their names, with the hope that the reader is intrigued enough to want to learn more. And as my Grandmother used to say, "You are judged by the company that you keep!" In her estimation, Reg would surely be judged as a great success for mankind and an example to follow.

We are living in an interesting period of world history. Movements in America are front and center and driving extreme change worldwide. Men of power (an oxymoronic statement as all men have a perceived systemic level of power over women either through physical or financial prowess), have been found placed on notice, and in some cases found criminally liable, that they can no longer exert their sexual desires over their female subordinates for quid pro quo compensation. White Americans and the world are "woke" to the fact that Black Lives Matter and they are marching in the streets in solidarity with African Americans to show their support. In the past "white privilege" could get a Black person hung, beaten to death, dragged behind a car or killed in a church bombing without repercussion. Now it can get its perpetrators arrested, tried, convicted, and sentenced (far too rare but true).

The coronavirus pandemic has held families captive in their living rooms to view the atrocities of Black men being murdered by White police officers and struggling to explain to their children that this is morally wrong and that these officers should be held legally accountable. The rights of gay and lesbian human beings are being expanded to provide equality in the workplace (two steps forward, one step back in some cases). All these things, though, were inevitable if you had a clear vision of how ineffective and unfair socioeconomic doctrines were enforced in our society. Reginald Petty saw this unfold, like the Guinea worms of intolerance that were discussed earlier. Here is his story……

# REFLECTIONS BY J.A. BROWN

In every family with which I am familiar, there is usually one designated child (either by blood or by choice), who will be anointed to curate the stories of the family. Elders speak to that young one, because, most often they sense the hunger in the questions of "What then?" and "Who was?" and "How did?" Quite often the stories are triggered by a photograph or an artifact sitting somewhere on a table or a shelf. Also, quite often the impulse to share happens as a meal is being prepared or room is being dusted, or a drive is being shared.

What a blessing that the "designated child" for this most necessary narrative has been there, making the season of discovery and sharing an opportunity to trace the history of Reginald Edwin Petty in a way that collects the bits and pieces of a life that has had an extraordinary impact on thousands of people, everywhere he has traversed and dwelt. Jaye P. Willis has done the work. We are grateful. And with this testimony, she shares with us the humility, grace, creativity, and perseverance by which Reginald Petty has influenced change and taught empowerment, from the neighborhood that is East St. Louis to the home he has made wherever he worked. The gifts he nurtured within himself he has shared prodigally, without limit – always with a determination that every human being he served would know that they were indeed gifts to the world. Because he said so.

Our mothers were classmates in high school and they never let that bond diminish or disappear. Often as a child, we drove to the Pettys' home, so that these friends could renew themselves and teach in the most powerful classroom imaginable – the living room, the kitchen, the front or back porch. And proving the mutuality by which true friendship is maintained, Helen Petty would come to Arralean Brown's home, so that they could continue to stoke the fire and warm themselves in assessing the world.

But back then there were no opportunities for him and me to interact or develop a similar bond. My family left East St. Louis during the great exodus (the 1950's) that is described within these pages. Because of the corrupt design of the economics of East St. Louis, "white flight" meant, first of all, corporate greed – which led to the abandonment of the industries that had kept the city stable for more than half a century. When the businesses either closed down or left, the people followed. No; *some* of the people followed. But here is a secret that is broadcast throughout this book: None of the people who migrated elsewhere were ever able to really leave home.

When my mother started her prayer campaign to bring her children back within the radius of a whisper, I found myself applying for a teaching and administrative position at Southern Illinois University in Carbondale. A few years after I had returned to the region, I got a telephone call from Reginald Petty. While he was in Washington DC, someone had given him a copy of my first poetry publication, *Accidental Grace*. When he looked at the biographical information at the end of the book, his charismatic skills went into overdrive. Why didn't we know each other? How did I manage to escape his scrutiny? And when could he drive to Carbondale to visit me? So now, the sons were carrying on the tradition of the mothers. We have driven back and forth, out of necessity – which is another aspect of true friendship and love. Throughout this book there are stories after story about how Reginald Petty has used that skill of connecting all of us, especially "the scattered," and reminding us that home is what we carry within us, what we rely on in times of doubt, loneliness, and fatigue.

Wherever he goes, Reginald Petty revives the downtrodden and abandoned and neglected. Rescuing books from the public library in East St. Louis is symbolic of how he has spent a lifetime rescuing dreams and youthful desires and aspirations in the hearts of his friends. He is a teacher, by word, by example and by calling. It could not be otherwise. He has built places where children could dream; where friends could be safe; and where any who were thirsting to remember why they had loved the city of East St. Louis, no matter what, could decide, "If Reginald can do it, I guess I can try, once more." His efforts to help found the East St. Louis Historical Society; his unparalleled contributions to the work of the 1917 East St. Louis Centennial Commission and his unwavering determination to see what he planted in the cultures where he has lived be brought to fruition and harvest -- he has never been anything less than a light shining in the darkness.

The author/curator/transcriber/archivist who presents this book to us is to be thanked. Much of that gratitude goes to her trusting in his encouragement. All of us who have known him can attest to what power that encouragement has been in our lives.

What this story proves so clearly is that Reginald Petty has made the world his home and has never doubted that he was prepared for his journey and his service because he drank deep from the fountain that has nourished so many. He guides us still.

Joseph A. Brown, SJ; Ph. D.

## INTRODUCTION BY REGINALD PETTY

(From a document he penned in 2007)

"I am writing an introduction without being sure what I am writing an introduction to. Over the years, friends and family have suggested that the experiences in my life are sufficiently unique and interesting enough to be of value to succeeding generations. A draft was begun in 1983 and it is currently 2007. This "document" began as an attempt to describe some of my "life shaping experiences" as a Black man living and working in America and Africa. Philosophical changes along the way would be included to relate experimental impact on my psyche and resulting behavior. It was decided early on that in order to understand the referred to experiences, it would be necessary to have some knowledge of my historical base. This includes the relevant history of my family, community, and the nation.

The concept of elders passing information on to the youth in both formal and informal ways exists in all cultures and is thousands of years old. In certain American ethnic and religious groups, processes exist for passing on information crucial to their continued existence. In fact, years were spent trying to determine what information would be most valuable. A listing of what can only be described as life shaping incidents and memories should serve as the underpinning. Hence, I spent considerable time reflecting on my past and bringing forth feelings to elicit my story."

Over the past five years, I have had very deep and meaningful conversations with Mr. Petty. In all instances, I have learned about life and humanity at his feet. This has singularly been one of the most revered relationships of my life, as I am also exposing and pouring my soul into this project. Meeting and speaking with his family and friends have been a joy and, in many cases, the takeaways have been eye-opening experiences. I adhered to this introduction as I crafted the book, in a manner to pay homage to his words. It is with a great sense of humility that I present to you the biography of Mr. Reginald Edwin Petty, as told to me, Mrs. Jaye Patrice Willis.

ONE SCORE

# Conceived Through Segregation

(Birth – 20) <u>1935-1955</u>

### *Haiku in Blue*

*A righteous spirit*
*Conceived through segregation*
*Blossoms in darkness*
—Jaye P. Willis

### *In the beginning...*

Even the most seemingly simple question to Reg turns into an indictment of the times. "Where were you born?" His response was poetic in nature. "I was conceived in East Saint Louis, Illinois but I was born in Saint Louis, Missouri." To understand why this statement is so powerful, I will need to give you some background on the region at the time.

Reginald Edwin Petty was born on October 7, 1935. His parents, Bruce Petty, and Helen Nicholson Petty resided in East Saint Louis but the hospitals in the city (St. Mary's and Christian Welfare) were segregated and would not allow Negro children to be born there. There were few options left for them, including midwifery or home delivery by a Negro doctor. The last option was to have their children in hospitals in Saint Louis, Missouri that allowed Negro births. Reg was born in the Negro section of Barnes Hospital in Saint Louis. It is important to note that the Mississippi River is the only mass that separates the two cities. It takes less than 15 minutes to travel across the bridge from the East Side to Barnes Hospital, but it is a trip marred by the bigotry and betrayal of the civil rights originally afforded to the black man when slavery was abolished. How more ironic that Missouri, the state where Dred Scott fought for his freedom from slavery, a state widely known for its heritage of slavery, became the last bastion for birthing black children in the region.

Reginald is the eldest of two sons. His younger brother, Bruce Anthony Petty, Jr., bears the name of his father. I asked Reginald if this was a practice of the times. His recollection centered on a conversation with his mother of his father not believing that the child she was carrying was his. His father would not give Reg his first name. That was all that he could remember of the circumstances. Of the things that he could remember, though, I received a royal history lesson of East St. Louis, as well as a deeper view into the soul of this man.

Reg readily recalls growing up in a small home in the Polack Town neighborhood, a segregated section of East St. Louis where many Polish immigrants lived. (The author contends that the word Polack is a derogatory term and does not mean to use it in that manner, but as a common point of reference in the city at the time.) In Polack Town, white people lived on certain blocks and black people lived on the others. He remembered at the ages of 3-5, living in four rooms with his parents, grandparents Carl and Georgia Smith, Aunt Lillian Smith, Cousin Frederick Boyd, and brother. His bed was in a cold room where two to three of them slept each night. There was a pot belly stove in the room next to his in which his grandparents slept. The adults sat around that stove and talked about the day's events as well as days of old - and the children listened. They had an outdoor toilet and a waterspout. He maintains vivid memories of the coal man and the ice man coming down the street announcing their arrival. Coal was shoveled down the home chute and blocks of ice were chopped up for the ice box (now known as a refrigerator). Even the Saturday night baths in the number 10 round tin tub were not forgotten. His father was a dark-skinned man while his mother was exceptionally light skinned.

Reg remembers the smell of chickens and ducks in the back yard. The family attended New Hope Church in the city, and he remembers sleeping on the front pew. This was a common phenomenon for young children attending Baptist and COGIC (Church of God in Christ) churches.

He also enjoyed sitting on the front porch and listening to the adults talk and gossip. One topic that left an indelible mark on Reg was discussion of the 1917 riots in East St. Louis. The number of colored people lynched, burned alive and otherwise killed that were reported in the newspapers was woefully low and underreported based on his elders' accounts. This event would factor in a major way later in his life.

Reg and Bruce grew up in a home where both parents worked. His father attended Howard University in Washington, DC and Illinois State University but never graduated. He accepted a position at the Aluminum Ore Company in East St. Louis in the chemistry department until the company left the city 20 years later. He was also highly active in the community, serving as a precinct committeeman.

Helen Nicholson Petty graduated from Illinois State College (now Illinois State University) with a two-year degree in Early Childhood Education. She taught remedial reading (her special interest) in the surrounding communities because back then you could not teach in East St. Louis if you were married. She taught at Lovejoy Elementary School, then Wilson Elementary School, where she was the only Black teacher educating an all-white student population. This situation did not change for 13 years

Reg remembers stories of his maternal great-great grandfather, Cozie Nicholson, being born of a white Frenchman and an African cook in 1820. Carl Smith was Georgia's second husband. Georgia Nicholson-Smith had four children with her first husband, Mr. Nicholson: daughters Helen and Lillian, and sons Jonathan and Cozie. They were all very active members at New Hope Baptist church. His mother's family was very strait-laced and staunch in almost everything they did. Children were expected to be always on their best behavior, neat, clean, mannerable and quiet. Fun was not often found in this environment. Reg's parents additionally did not display public affection, either for each other or their children.

His father's family was from Alabama. His paternal grandparents were Isaiah (sometimes listed as Isaac) and Jessie Beatrice Battle Petty. They had nine children – Florence, Stella, William, Bruce, Melvin, Glenn, Lorene, Christine and Arletha. His grandfather worked as a Section Hand on the Southern Railroad in East St. Louis. This side of the family was much more fun to be around. He remembers the holidays especially, where his grandmother and her daughters were cooking. The food was always great and comforting, like love.

## Off to the races...

Reg recalled a bus ride with his parents when he was about five years old. A white person looked at him and his mother and asked him what color they were. He told her his father was a Negro, but he and his mother were white. At this point in his life, he only viewed race by sight, as many still do today. He soon after learned what his place in the society of the 1940s and beyond in America would be. That misperception on his part is more comical now.

Even clothes shopping brought attention to race in his younger years. He remembers shopping with his parents one day, seeing that colored people could not try on clothes and shoes without purchasing them first. However, white people could try on clothes before buying them. At an early age, he found this insulting, yet his parents had been desensitized to this phenomenon and found it "normal".

The two major parks in the city were Grand Marais and Cahokia Mounds. The latter was created by American Indians and was of tremendous archeological significance. Colored children were not allowed to climb the mounds, but they would sneak over to slide down them on sleds. There was a small section for colored folks to have picnics, but they could not cross the borders. Grand Marais also had a Negro section.

Reg remembers the movie theatres in the city then. The Majestic Theatre was the largest of the five whites-only theaters in the city. The

Negro theatres were the Broadway, the Harlem, and the Deluxe. When Reg was in grade school, he remembers going to the movies to see *Magnificent Obsession,* and it would change his life forever. The movie is about a Doctor who learned to use his skills and finances to assist people without knowing they were being helped by him. This positively stuck with Reg and became his mantra. After seeing the movie, he took small amounts of money he had and gave them to people without them knowing. He would slip change in someone's pocket or mailbox if they were in need. He did not have much, but his parents used to say, "Every little bit helps." This experience helped him to continue doing this the rest of his life, whether in his studies, social work, or similar activities, he would find ways to improve the human species on this planet.

## *Grade School*

Reg and Bruce would attend Crispus Attucks School in Polack Town. It is fascinating how even the naming of schools epitomized segregation in the city. All the children and teachers were Negro, as was Crispus Attucks. A bright point to extrapolate from this phenomenon was the history of the school's namesake. Crispus Attucks was an American stevedore of African and Native American descent, widely regarded as the first person killed in the Boston Massacre and thus the first American killed in the American Revolution. Knowledge of the life of Crispus Attucks would benefit children of all races but was seemingly relegated to the education of Negro children in the city. The deployment of the separate but equal doctrine, confirmed by the US Supreme Court in their *Plessy vs Ferguson* decision of 1896, was in full effect in East St. Louis during Reg's formal education. Reg remembers studying hard to maintain good grades while in school, as his family valued education. Having a Mother as a schoolteacher was also motivation. As a youth, Reg used to wonder if this was a blessing or a curse. Note: As the industries that made East St. Louis a booming town began to leave, the White citizens also began leaving the city for neighboring towns like Belleville and Lebanon. The introduction of integration of schools was also occurring and schools like Attucks were abandoned, though the structure still stands today.

## **High School**

Reg would attend the only Black high school in the city, Lincoln Senior High School. There were other high schools, including an all-male parochial one called Central Catholic High School (later renamed Assumption High School in 1953) and the all-white East St. Louis Senior High School. Some youth living in the city section known as Fireworks Station were bused to Lovejoy High School in Lovejoy, Illinois, bypassing Lincoln and some eight miles north of East St. Louis. The rationale for this was that Lincoln was overcrowded and the next nearest all-black high school was Lovejoy.

As with most young men, Reg was fascinated by the fast lifestyle of the hustlers in his community. As in today's times, their lives tend to seem more glamorous than most, as you often see them in the finest clothes, the fanciest cars, and with the prettiest women. But as the proverb goes, "all that glitters is not gold". Once, while attending Lincoln Senior High school, he became enamored with a local street hustler who had a nice car.

While walking home one day, the hustler noticed Reg and asked him if he wanted a ride. As a young man of small stature, Reg was excited that this larger-than-life cat noticed him. He got in the car and saw several other guys inside. While driving along, another car pulled up and the drivers began arguing. The arguing escalated to a fight as both cars emptied, and the drivers began swinging at one another. Reg had not been so close to gang warfare before and was sure that he was going to either be hurt very badly or killed. As the fight escalated, a police car pulled up and made the youth line up against their cars. After frisking them and searching for other incriminating evidence, Reg and several others were let free to go home.

Reg did not necessarily view this as a "scared straight" moment but as one of the exhilarating moments of his life. He was in the thick of the action, watching life go on around him, almost consuming him. Nothing about his size or color mattered and he was ready to fight to the death with those he stood with. He had been prepared for this moment. This event would be the catalyst to the strength, courage, and fight of the man that this book is about.

## *The Athlete Within*

Sports were extremely popular at Lincoln. Lincoln would become renown throughout the state and country for the athletic prowess of their male and female athletes. While attending Lincoln, Reg played basketball and ran track for the school. While playing in a basketball game, he fainted and had his first brain seizure. These seizures would continue throughout his life. He would stop playing basketball because of them but continued to run track, becoming the captain of the team in his senior year.

Reg ran track along with good friend Theodore 'Ted' Savage, who would go on to national prominence as a sports legend, playing for several major league baseball teams, including the St. Louis Cardinals. Reg also played baseball with several of his closest friends, including James "Big Monk" Currie and Willie "Lil Monk" Currie. "Lil Monk" was widely regarded as one of the best baseball players to play in the city while Ted was highly regarded for his basketball prowess. Reg enjoyed track and was a rather good runner.

During the mid to late 1950s, the sports competitions in Metro St. Louis were as segregated as the schools, so Lincoln primarily competed against the Negro St. Louis high schools like Vashon, Sumner, and Central. Reg competed against Sumner great Dick Gregory, who would later become a world-renowned comedian and civil rights activist. One of the most important things to come from his time as an athlete at Lincoln is the lifelong friendships he would make. They were gentleman athletes who dressed in shirts, ties and trousers when traveling to competitions. Reg understood that as a man dresses, so he acts. He has carried that demeanor with him throughout his life.

Segregation and racism showed up at each event with white runners, as Reg and his fellow Black teammates were not allowed to dress with the white teams or even use the same toilets. The officials even changed their times in favor of their white counterparts. This injustice and inequity permeated his consciousness and elevated his desire to do something to eradicate this social norm.

*Jaye P. Willis*

## College Life (Undergrad Years)

Reg graduated from Lincoln at the age of 16. He received a partial scholarship to attend the University of Illinois in Champaign. In the early 1950's, any Illinois high school graduate was automatically accepted into the University of Illinois. He was a little apprehensive to leave home at such a young age, but the challenge of higher education positively motivated him. He also wanted to make his parents and family proud of him. His parents did not have much money to send with him but were able to send him $5.00 per week to help with his expenses. Reg found a job in the school cafeteria and as a cleaning man at several white fraternity houses on campus. He remarked that the frat boys always had lots of food and alcohol to drink. He would often eat after serving and cleaning, which helped him save money. Friends and fellow East St. Louisans would also look after him. Reg joined Kappa Alpha Psi Fraternity, Incorporated and lived in the fraternity house on campus.

Ted Savage would also attend the University of Illinois at Champaign on a basketball scholarship. Ted and the other blacks on the team were natural talents but had a flair for playing "street ball". Though effective, it was not as refined as the white coach wanted. Comments were reportedly made that the black athletes would have to stop playing "nigger ball" if they wanted to remain on the team. Ted would spend one year at U of I (an affectionate name for the flagship school of the state of Illinois) and then transfer to Lincoln University in Jefferson City, Missouri, one of the historically black colleges and universities (HBCU) in the United States. It was his friendship with Ted and others that helped Reg adjust to life on his own in a perversely racist system.

Reg recalled having to take a swimming class at U of I where the teacher was extremely strict. He would routinely take points off Reg's scores and give him lower grades without merit. Reg watched as his counterparts would receive higher grades for doing the same or worse than he. He understood that his scholarship was tied to his maintaining a certain grade point average and that flunking this course, which was not instrumental to his becoming a social worker, could turn the tide on his education. He would ultimately pass the class with the lowest grade he ever received.

To identify balance in his life, he looked for a church home in Champaign. His roots were with New Hope Baptist Church, an all-Black church featuring Black music. He could not find such a place in his adopted city, so he joined a Unitarian Church. He found the religious teachings more satisfying as their goal was to assist the individual to find their religious selves. The services varied from Christian, Buddhist, and Arabic services. He would continue to maintain a membership in the Unitarian Church throughout his life.

On a visit home, after being fully immersed in the racial tide of Champaign, he questioned why his Black friends were listening to the Amos and Andy radio program. The performers were two White men pretending to be the most offensive and stereotypical versions of Black people imaginable. They frequently spoke negatively about the Black community. There were other programs like this on the radio, showcasing Blacks as stupid, ignorant, and shiftless, all while being portrayed by White people. Even some early television shows, like The Amos and Andy Show, showcased Black folks playing these roles! And the Jack Benny show, where Eddie Rochester played a buffoonish Black role, was soulfully offensive to Reg. After stating this, Reg recalled that the most negative comment one Black man could say to another was to call him a Black Motherfucker. He was calling all of them that at that moment!

Reg transferred to Southern Illinois University at Carbondale, known as SIU, for the beginning of his junior year. He would rejoin his friend, Dick Gregory, at SIU, where he hoped the racism would be less prominent. "If hopes and dreams were peaches and cream…" At this point, though, he felt that he had the necessary skills to navigate the racism and become successful. For a little historical perspective, in 1954, the tuition at SIU was $28.50 per quarter, including books, and $15.00 per quarter for housing. The President of the University seemed interested in integrating students into the campus facilities and activities. Reg had a European roommate, which surprised him and the roommate! At the Student Union, Black students sat in the same place. The University President moved all the chairs from that location to another place. He wanted the Black students to become a genuine part of the community, though neither of the student groups wanted that at the time.

Reg and other Black students went to nearby Culp, Illinois, to attend a party. The band there played blues music. Both Black and Whites attended the party, though interracial dancing was not allowed, as that action could lead to future problems. A rope was placed down the middle of the floor, with Blacks on one side and Whites on the other, listening to the same music. At the time, Reg did not find this particularly strange as this was a way to avoid violence. Both groups were interested in listening to good music, and that was good enough, for then.

Reg with SIUC Kappalier Group circa 1954

Reg and a group of friends formed a rhythm and blues quartet called the Kappaliers. They won several amateur contests, and he became quite popular on campus, particularly with the fairer sex.

He met a beautiful young woman on campus named Alma Marr. They married right after Reg graduated from SIU with a Bachelor's degree in Sociology.

"Alma was a very attractive, light skinned young woman with a cute nose", recalls Bessie Peabody, a lifelong friend of Reg. He and Bessie grew up and attended school together. "Alma was also very nice and sweet and always wore her hair in a bob style. She was from Mounds, Illinois, and a member of Alpha Kappa Alpha Sorority, Incorporated."

Parents Bruce and Helen Petty. Photo from Petty archive.

Mom Helen Nicholson Petty. Photo from Petty archive.

Young Reginald with parents. Photo from Petty archives.

Petty's family home. Photo from Petty archives.

Jaye P. Willis

Beta Chapter, Kappa Alpha Psi Fraternity, Incorporated. University of Illinois, Champaign-Urbana circa 1952. Photo found on Internet.

Gamma Upsilon Chapter, Kappa Alpha Psi Fraternity, Incorporated. Southern Illinois University, Carbondale, Illinois circa 1954. Photo found on Internet.

*Jaye P. Willis*

## **Out of Character**
### *By Reginald Petty*

Who we are
Lying down across graves of our ancestors
Absorbing their chi
Still learning from them even after their deaths
Dancing flowers, pressing forward
What is there for us to give but what we are given?
What is there to teach, but what we are taught?
The only love that blossoms forth from us is generations old
We find a place for ourselves in ourselves
Our totality, our ancestors, judged by all who passed before
Limitless knowledge, limitless love
If we but ask, if the drums ask for us
If the arts ask for us if the unspoken words ask for us
If our friends ask for us if our family asks for us
If the community asks for us
Our past selves always ask for us
CAN WE LISTEN?

# TWO SCORE

# Transplanting Knowledge

**(21-40)** 1956-1975

### *Gift Giver*

*Vaporous soldier*
*Traverses distant homelands*
*Transplanting knowledge*
—Jaye P. Willis

Armed with his bachelor's degree and wife Alma, Reg returned to East St. Louis to begin a new journey in his education. Reg and Alma moved in with his parents, creating another branch to their extended family. Soon afterwards a son, Bruce Anthony Petty, affectionately known as Tony, was born. Reg began teaching at an elementary school and later a junior high school in East St. Louis. Though he loved helping to mold young minds, he felt that he needed to expand his education to better serve the children and his family. He also needed more money. After a year of teaching, Reg applied for graduate school. He moved his family to Rockford, IL where he began a career as a Social Worker. Still striving to increase his knowledge, he moved the family to Chicago, where he began working on his graduate degree in Social Work at the University of Chicago.

Chicago is a fascinating city, full of music, food, diversity, culture, and life. Reg was drawn to the music of Chicago and took several gigs as a session drummer for Chess Records, playing for such Blues greats as Muddy Waters and John Lee Hooker. He became enraptured with the night life and the goings on with these musicians as it brought a bit of home back to him. East St. Louis was known for its bustling night life. Neighboring St. Louis, Missouri closed around midnight and many of its counties were "dry" on Sunday (meaning they did not sell liquor). East St. Louis was open practically all night. Patrons and renowned musicians like Ike Turner and Albert King would travel across the bridge to Illinois to jam until dawn.

## *Influences*

To make ends meet, Reg became employed at a Jewish Community Center in Hyde Park, IL, working within an interracial environment. He was also introduced to the African American Heritage Association (AAHA), whose goal was to "…raise the level of self-esteem in Black people through a more accurate and increased knowledge of the history of African kingdoms, especially focusing on Egypt and Ethiopia". Reg became a pivotal player in the AAHA, ultimately serving as the Chicago Council AAHA President, while leading efforts to showcase the group and raise the consciousness of the people of Chicago through the enforcement of Black Pride. The *Chicago Daily Defender (National edition) (1921-1967)*; July 14, 1962; ProQuest Historical Newspaper: Chicago Defender (1910-1975) pg. 4, ran an article entitled "Chicago to Celebrate DuSable Week, Aug. 19-25" in which this excerpt appeared:

> "…Chicago Council AAHA President Petty declared "Only anti-Africanism, rationalized by lies about race to make possible anti-human discrimination, segregation, and Jim Crow, can explain the failure of the citizenry of Chicago to give appropriate

recognition and honor to the city's first settler. By establishing the annual DuSable Week, the AAHA is affording the city's fathers and the Catholic Archdiocese to make amends for practically burying and ignoring the city's first settler and illustrious Catholic of African descent that founded one of the foremost cities and industrial complexes in the world. Our organization feels certain that the whole city will be appreciative of its proposals in honor of Chicago's first settler."…"

For those unfamiliar with Jean Baptiste Pointe du Sable, he is regarded as the first permanent non-indigenous settler of what would become known as Chicago, Illinois, and regarded as the "Founder of Chicago." He was a Black man.

The AAHA would go on to establish more culturally enriched community activities, including Negro History Week which was proclaimed by Mayor Richard J. Daley on February 12-19, 1961. The Chicago Daily Defender reported that the AAHA was sponsor of the week and cited this excerpt from the proclamation:

"…governmental agencies are engaged in a continuing fight against discrimination and efforts to promote greater harmony among people of all races and creeds."

Reg would go on to serve in a leadership position with the AAHA for several years in the early 1960's. Whether serving on a delegation that traveled to Springfield, Illinois to petition then Governor Kerner against the proposed cut in welfare checks or being a guest speaker at numerous community forums directed at uplifting citizens, particularly citizens of color, with topics like "What It Means To Walk Together", Reg truly earned that title recently attributed to a young Barack Obama some 40 years later in the same city – Community Organizer!

In his early days with the AAHA, Reg was immersed in African politics as the group participated in the July 1960 Inaugural Banquet of the American Negro Emancipation Centennial in Chicago where Ghanaian officials represented their commerce department at the International Trade Fair. The next month, in a letter to United Nations

Secretary General Dag Hammarskjold, the AAHA went on record in support of the government of the Congo headed by Premier Patrice Lumumba. Reg travelled to the Republic of the Congo with a delegation of AAHA members to meet Premier Lumumba. Unbeknownst to Reg, he was setting himself up for his future posts in Africa. Continuing his desire to address the international concerns of Black folks, he and several others travelled to Cuba to meet with Fidel Castro on this subject. This was a particularly tricky situation in the 1960's as the infamous Bay of Pigs invasion had empowered the Cuban government and strained relationships with the United States. What he knew and believed was that he had made moves that uplifted and supported the Black community in Chicago, even to the point of putting himself in physical danger because of his words and deeds.

Alice Windom, a civil rights activist and close friend of Maya Angelou, shared a time back in the late 1950's when she and Reg attended a meeting where some "controversial" discussions on the state of race in America were discussed. Though neither she nor Reg joined nor were otherwise affiliated with this group, just being in the room would later raise concern by the federal government. Alice shared the following "… the secretary for the group was taking minutes but was also sharing the notes with government spies who were keeping tabs on such groups. It was common that if there was a group of Blacks discussing the current state of Black affairs in America, then one of them was a snitch for the government. You had to be very careful back then on what you said and to whom…"

He spent many evenings speaking with the Black Muslims from a nearby school. This would become a key moment in his life. He would meet and become lifelong friends and a confidante to Malcolm X, an audacious community organizer who would become the revered leader of the Nation of Islam. Though Reg never converted to the Muslim or Islamic faith, he admired Malcolm's mind and his desire to reignite Black pride in their communities. Reg was now engaging in cross-cultural interactions and discussions where everyone was respected for their individual contributions. He listened, observed, and expanded his mind on race relations at the time. He attended various focus meetings where race relations and socioeconomic disparities were discussed. He knew even better that more work needed to be done to improve society in America. He began to realize his purpose. A purpose that would mean uncomfortable times, danger, arrests, and possible death. Alma did not share this vision with Reg, opting for a more stable and mainstream life with their family. Alma and Reg divorced, with Tony going with his mother.

Reg would end his time in Chicago and the university to go back to SIU Carbondale to complete his Master of Social Work degree. He experienced a tremendous number of life-altering events over the next five years which were critical to him, the State of Illinois, and the individuals that he would encounter.

SIU was a familiar place to him with established relationships. It would also bring him closer to his son. As Reg began to pick up his life in Carbondale, he was again noticed by the female population. Though interracial dating was unheard of in Southern Illinois, Reg dated several white women, including one from France and one from England.

During one Christmas at SIU, Reg found himself attending a Black church in the city, reconnecting him with that population. One of his professors gave him a graduate assistantship which covered his tuition and provided a small stipend for living expenses. He found himself living with four White male students, also graduate assistants. It was a unique experience for them all, and one that they all value to this day. That Christmas was spent together in their home, cooking, and sharing a variety of food. Afterwards, they went to a bar which they found very satisfactory and completed their final bonding. From then on, most of his life would be spent in integrated situations.

## *Living His Truth*

One of his graduate assistant projects was working on a contract with the Child Welfare Department to conduct a statewide research assessment to determine the value of modifying the current policies regarding adoption throughout the state. Policies made it impossible for blacks or minorities to adopt due to the standards being too high (income and numerous other factors). He found many of those policies to be unnecessary, like the size of the house, room space, and the education of the parents to raise a family. The assessment took a year, and the necessary changes were made to bring the policies in place for equitable adoptions. Already, he was a game changer for the orphaned and disenfranchised.

Reg was a research assistant on another project. The Sociology department was tasked to collect all computer data using modern techniques (at the time). He made himself available to all departments, with Dr. Brooks being his main professor. During this time, he visited Mississippi and Alabama to analyze voter registration issues in the South. Based on his findings, he joined several groups involved in improving the process for Black voting, including the Student Nonviolent Coordinating Committee (SNCC). Over the next few years, he maintained a second home outside of Jackson, Mississippi, recalling:

> "One day I was sitting outside of a lady's home drinking a Coca-Cola and talking with her about registering to vote. I sat the bottle down next to me. White police officers arrested me for littering and took me to a white barbershop where they shaved my head. During this degrading act, their discussion was on how ignorant and unstable Blacks are by coming to Mississippi and Alabama to register Blacks to vote! I had to keep from laughing as I almost had my master's degree while the White folks talking barely had a Sixth-grade education!"

During his time in Mississippi registering Blacks to vote, Reg was arrested over 30 times. At the time, he believed that was a record number of arrests for an individual for voter registration. He also fell victim to some of the most heinous brutalization inflicted on a man at the hand of those sworn to protect and serve. This would not be the first or the last time that his life was placed on the line in support of others. I often wondered if Reg had a death wish because of the situations he continued to place himself in for others. I now see that he, like all great people who strive to make substantive changes in the human condition, are selfless in following their hearts and minds to achieving their life's purpose.

Reg became a lifelong friend with a young man who also worked with voter registration efforts, including being one of the original Freedom Riders and a leader in SNCC. His name was John Lewis. He would become a U.S. Congressman from the state of Georgia and serve for over 30 years. Reg also met with friends and confidantes Dr. Martin Luther King, Jr. and Stokely Carmichael, who succeeded John Lewis as the leader of SNCC, because he was having doubts if the programs being established would be successful based on the economics of the communities. Blacks could vote in some situations, but employment was still difficult and unequal. He would participate in many meetings of the mind with high-ranking officials in the civil rights movement as his personality and drive matched theirs.

Once, while visiting Mounds, Illinois, Reg suffered a seizure. The people he was with took him to a local hospital, but that hospital did not admit Black people. They had to pass several hospitals to get him back to the hospital in Carbondale. This disparity in life saving treatment based solely on the color of the skin of a person only fueled his desire to strive to eradicate racial perceptions and injustices. After hearing this story, I was struck with a sense of grief – what would have happened to all the people that Reg positively impacted over his lifetime if he had died from this incident. The world would have been deprived of his gifts! Luckily, there was a plan for this man put in place by One who has power over our frailties.

This biography does not mean to paint Reginald Petty as a saint. Not by any means. He also had his frailties. Reg was approached by one of his professors and asked a very frank question – "Do you know anyone who can perform an abortion?" At the time, all his professors except for one were White. Reg said he knew someone in St. Louis, but it had to be early in the pregnancy (first three months). At the request of a professor, Reg took a young lady to have an abortion performed. This "favor" resulted in several other professors coming to him to ask for the same service. He did not think much of it at the time, so he continued for seven or eight more times. The doctor thought all the girls were Reg's lady friends, as they were all white females. Reg began to feel uncomfortable with the whole process and he told the professors that he would no longer like to do this. He did, however, introduce them to the doctor, who only charged $150 for the service. This chink in his armor weighs heavily on Reg's mind even today.

While working in the mail room for one of the dormitories, Reg was drawn to a particular lovely young lady named Lucy Klaus. She was also studying Sociology. Lucy recalled that Reg spoke in a very low voice. She smiled as she said "All the White girls liked him. He was like a father/confessor." She was from a small all-white town in southern Illinois. Reg was now approaching 30 years of age and was working as an assistant to several professors on campus. He was a man of influence which made him even more attractive. Lucy recalled flirting with him while he was working in the mailroom on campus.

When he and Lucy decided that they wanted to get married, Reg approached her father, but he was not happy with the arrangement. He knew the problems that they would face as an interracial couple in America in the 1960's. Taken aback by her father's disapproval, Reg reached out to his good friend and SIU classmate Dick Gregory, who supported Reg on the matter and offered to speak with Lucy's father on Reg's behalf. By this time, Dick had made a name for himself as a professional comedian and civil rights activist by being the first Black performer to sit on the infamous couch on the Jack Parr show. Dick spoke with Lucy's father, as Reg imagined in the same provocative tone he used every day, to plead Reg's case. After that call, Reg and Lucy were married. It was 1965.

Lucy was a case worker with Public Aid in Illinois. Prior to their marriage, Reg, and Lucy, along with friends Gene Martin, Collin Reynolds, and Harland Randolph, went to Breckinridge, Kentucky to start one of the first Job Corps Centers in the United States. Per Reg, SIU had the contract to establish the Center and the government selected the site; a closed military base which they were able to secure at no cost. Reg recalls that Breckinridge was a very segregated area. Once, he and Lucy went into town to purchase clothes for her. She wanted his opinion on her selections. The store people were furious, staring at them and ultimately asking them to leave. He also recalled taking their car to be repaired but when they returned, it was damaged by local technicians.

Despite these incidents, they forged ahead with the Job Corps Center, which would introduce him to greater opportunities to serve.

One day, out of the blue, Reg was contacted by US politician and diplomat Sargent Shriver, Jr., who was working with his brother-in-law, sitting President of the United States John F. Kennedy, to apply for a position with a newly created organization called the United States Peace Corps. The Peace Corps mission is to promote world peace and friendship by fulfilling three goals:

> To help the people of interested countries in meeting their need for trained men and women;
>
> To help promote a better understanding of Americans on the part of the peoples served;
>
> To help promote a better understanding of other peoples on the part of the Americans.

Of course, the vetting process for acceptance into this diplomatic post is extensive. The Federal Bureau of Investigation (FBI) led the investigations of potential candidates for these posts. Reg remembers sitting in the office of FBI Director J. Edgar Hoover who challenged him on the specifics of meetings he attended, trips he had taken, people he had spoken with, etc. Reg even recalled being threatened by Mr. Hoover to make false accusations about New York State Assemblywoman Shirley Chisholm in exchange for getting the Peace Corps appointment. That man seemed to know a great deal about Reg's life which led to the question: "Who's talking about me?" Based on the "controversial" accounts written so far in this biography, it was no surprise that Reg was not selected on his first application. However, after speaking with Sargent Shriver and President Kennedy, Reg was appointed to his first post in the Peace Corps, and it would be in Africa, though several years later.

Jaye P. Willis

# Peace Corps – *Upper Volta*

Reg's first Peace Corps assignment was in the West African Country of Upper Volta in the early fall of 1967. Upper Volta, now known as Burkina Faso, had recently obtained independence from France in 1960 and maintained French as its primary language. Reg is fluent in the French language. Upper Volta was known as the poorest country in the world at the time, with an average income of $30 per year. It was also noted for practicing female circumcision.

His first Peace Corps Director would be Tom Fox. Tom was the Country Director in Togo before getting the assignment in Upper Volta. He and Reg had spoken over the phone that summer before meeting. Tom had never heard of Reg but instantly took a liking to him. According to Tom, Reg became his Deputy Country Director in Upper Volta on September 20, 1967. The Country program had about 50 Peace Corps volunteers. The volunteers served in two-year rotations (maximum three years) with a subsistence allowance and a small amount put into a "readjustment account" for the end of their service.

Reg worked principally with the volunteers, who were comprised of approximately two-thirds White mainly from Ivy League schools and four Black. He led a group of 20 volunteers working with the local inhabitants digging wells in a dry part of the country. The wells had to be 10 feet deep to get to the water which was used for drinking and irrigation. The soil was 'laterite', meaning it turned to rock once it was plowed. With only three or four rainfalls throughout the year, and no indication when they would happen, it made the job even more imperative. The Upper Voltans would pray to the god Intenata to provide rain. One of the byproducts of polluted water sources was known as Guinea worms, defined as "… a long, threadlike nematode of tropical Asia and Africa that is a subcutaneous parasite of humans and other mammals and causes ulcerative lesions on the legs and feet." Once fully developed, these parasites, sometimes growing up to 12 inches long, exit the body through the skin in a painful manner. **Purifying the water removes guinea worms.** Reg's philosophy early on was to "teach and not just do" for the people he would serve so that they could sustain themselves in the long run.

Tom and Reg immediately hit it off as they had similar interests – music, sports, and Africa. Tom was comfortable with their relationship and with the volunteers. Their conversations were very frank about black/white issues and they easily discussed racial matters. Tom and Reg spent about two-thirds of the time working in the capital city of Ouagadougou. They traveled together a lot and frequently visited each other's homes over the two years that they worked together. Tom found Reg to be a good friend, colleague, and person. Tom had no concerns about Reg's interracial marriage, though he had never seen one in the United States. He never saw any issues with Reg and Lucy's marriage and found himself more progressive than that. Lucy and Reg told Tom about a church in Washington, DC that they liked. Tom and his wife joined that church and are still members today. When Tom completed his two-year rotation as Country Director, Reg would become one of the first Black Peace Corps Country Directors, still in Upper Volta. Following their time in Upper Volta, Tom and Reg would see each other about every 6-7 years. Conference calls were held periodically with the former volunteers and the Country Directors to keep in touch and share fond memories. Tom would go on to become a Regional Director of Peace Corps for Africa.

Lucy shared that Reg is not defined by color or race. While living in Upper Volta, they were treated more like people than a couple. There was loose ignorance or maybe an unfamiliar cultural shift on behalf of the young couple. Once, when Lucy had to return to the United States for a personal matter, the African housekeeper told her not to worry and that she would take on her duties as Reg's wife until she returned. This was the custom for this community and was a proper responsibility. Lucy in no uncertain terms expressed that this cultural observance was not welcomed or warranted! Reg found the entire episode very amusing. This misunderstanding occurs when cultural relativism is employed, or simply when one tries to impart their societal views on another culture.

Jaye P. Willis

## ***Back in the USA, Round 1...***

Reg returned to the United States around 1971, after serving as the U. S. Peace Corps Country Director in Upper Volta and working as a consultant in East Africa. He began to work consistently with his close friend and confidante David Levine, initially at General Learning Corporation. David would become the Director of Programming and Training for the Peace Corps at the end of 1977, working with 55-60 Country Directors. David and Reg worked together again during David's third term with the Peace Corps, where he had earlier been a Peace Corps volunteer and staff member in Ethiopia. They overlapped two years while Reg worked in Swaziland and Kenya and then became consultants working in Egypt.

Reg and David found that they had very few ideological differences. David confided to me that he learned a lot from Reg, but mainly that it is imperative to use dual lenses of class and race when viewing racism. Reg was also very liberal and astute at using political strategy. David was more impetuous, but this characteristic served him well. He thought Reg was extraordinarily insightful and wise and most admired his commitments, honesty, and knowledge. He was also enamored with Reg's warmth and how he dealt with him as a person. They too liked sports and were drawn by their intellect. David had also heard of Reg from his former colleagues at Breckenridge before meeting him.

David and Reg were in Washington, DC during the DC Black Power Structure, an era when Black Americans were gaining prominence in business and politics in DC. Reg was a friend and confidante to Mayor Marion Barry, the second mayor of Washington, DC, who was most famous for being the first prominent Civil Rights activist to become chief executive of a major American city and most infamous for his brushes with the law on drug charges. More will be said on Reg and Marion's relationship in an upcoming section. David was working in DC, occasionally consulting with Reg's brother Bruce, as a Housing Consultant. Bruce was a very accomplished man in his own right. He was also a graduate of SIU with a BS in Chemistry and minor in Business in 1962. In 1974, he earned his Master of Business Administration from Howard University in Washington, DC, fulfilling the legacy his father began. Bruce worked in Madrid, Spain as a chemistry teacher at the International High School and later became an Executive Vice-President with A.L. Nellum & Associates in Washington, DC.

Bruce Anthony Petty. Photo from Petty archives.

Though both born in October, Reg's astrological sign is Libra, with the trait of being very diplomatic, natural peacemakers, and expert at being tactful in their relationships. David is a Scorpio, with the traits of being very focused, brave, loyal, faithful, and ambitious. I asked David when he first developed a sense of trust with Reg. He recalled an incident in a DC bar where he and Reg were having drinks. David was smaller in stature than Reg and was being harassed by a bar patron who was much larger than him. Reg promptly got in the guy's face and said, "Touch him and I will kill you!" Reg sounded very convincing and the guy backed down, though knowing Reg it is very doubtful that he would have taken that exact action. Growing up in "the hood" gives one the street swag to lay down a strong bluff to a lame fool. Translation, when one is raised in an inner-city environment; one understands the value of obtaining a daunting personality to instill fear in an opponent during a face-to-face confrontation. Both men were working for the African Development Corporation (ADC) in 1981 and 1982. These two men are so in tune in their beliefs that when the ADC abandoned its founding principles, they both resigned from their positions.

Left to right, Petty, James Garrett, Angela Davis and Stokely Carmichael. Photo in the National Museum of African American History and Culture. Copyright Milton Williams archives

David was not surprised that Reg married a white woman. Reg and Lucy raised their children internationally in Africa, emphasizing that they be raised as Black Americans. They were attended to by a Black African housekeeping staff, which was normal in Africa as people worked with each other to assist in getting through daily chores and activities. David is still in touch with Lucy today.

David stated with conviction that Reg was inadequately known for his civil rights movement leadership. He further said the following related to Reg's influence in the civil rights movement… "He (Reg) was near the top and not a passing fancy. Reg is quiet and unassuming and valued for what he said and did." Reg knew and worked with many of the big names, including Dr. Martin Luther King, Jr., John Lewis, Jesse Jackson, and Malcom X, even serving as an advisor to several of them. He is knowledgeable about civil rights events as he participated in many of them, including the march across the infamous Edmund Pettus Bridge in Selma, Alabama, where he was working with SNCC and Stokely Carmichael at the time.

As an aside, upon walking through the National Museum of African American History and Culture in Washington, DC in February of 2017,

I came across a picture of Reg with Angela Davis, Stokely Carmichael and another unidentified gentleman circa 1966.

Both Reg and the gentleman next to him were listed as unidentified in the photo. I showed the picture to Reg and he confirmed that it was he on the far left. I could not allow that to go uncorrected. While working with Dr. William Shannon, Curator of the St. Clair County Historical Society (of which I serve on the Board of Directors), he was able to provide me with the contacts that I needed at the NMAAHC to send a correction for the photo. The NMAAHC DigiTeam researched my information and also provided the name of the man standing next to Reg as Mr. James Garrett. A formal update was made to the record. I received approval from the owner of the photograph, Mr. Milton Williams, to use the photograph in this book. I was so very proud to be able to do this for Reg. How exhilarating too!

## Impactful Leadership

Another compatriot of Reg is Daniel Rafferty, a former Peace Corps volunteer in Turkey. Daniel was born in Rock Island, Illinois and is a graduate of the University of Illinois, in Champaign. It's no coincidence that these two became friends, as their physical life journeys crossed paths, even though in different years.

Dan met Reg in 1970 after Reg had completed his first tour with the Peace Corps in Upper Volta. Reg had returned to Washington, DC and was working with the General Learning Corporation (GLC). Dan was a 5th grade teacher in Anacostia, a suburb of Washington, DC, when he saw a federal bid with the GLC for a training program for the fall of 1969. Dan had previously done this type of work in Turkey, which consisted of micro-training (10-minute training bits) focused on inner-city assistance. One area was working with young Black mothers without college degrees to bring them into the elementary schools and read to the children. This experience would then lead them to teacher's aide and teacher positions. This was linked to other federally funded programs like the Ocean Hill, Brooklyn-Brownsville Community Outreach programs.

After a year of working in Washington, DC, Reg was asked to work with training AmeriCorps Volunteers in Service to America (VISTA) under the GLC contract. Reg was responsible for the Atlanta, Boston and Washington, DC training centers. The DC groups included Puerto Rico and the US Virgin Islands. VISTA and Americorps were later merged under ACTION, a US Government agency described as "the federal domestic volunteer agency" in 1971 under President Richard Nixon. Other agencies incorporated into ACTION included the Peace Corps, and various programs under the Office of Economic Opportunity (OEO).

It was during Reg's leadership position in New York that he reunited with a longtime friend from East St. Louis. Her name was Barbara Ann Teer. Barbara was a beautiful and sophisticated woman making her mark as a dancer in the Big Apple. Back in East St. Louis, her parents were movers and shakers in the community in both politics and real estate. Barbara Ann was just ending her marriage to accomplished actor Godfrey Cambridge and was being courted by such elite men as actor Robert Hooks, Sr., and prolific trumpeter Miles Davis. Enter a young recent college graduate from Oberlin College with a degree in Politics and International Studies – Mr. Michael Lythcott, who would be intimately influenced by several accomplished, educated, and iconic citizens of East St. Louis, Illinois while living in New York, New York!

Oberlin College, in Oberlin, Ohio, is described as a private liberal arts college and conservatory of music. It is the oldest coeducational liberal arts college in the United States and the second oldest continuously operating coeducational institute of higher learning in the world. While studying at Oberlin College, one of Michael's professors was the distinguished Eugene Redmond, a professor of English literature who hails from East St. Louis, Illinois (Encounter #1). Michael had made a pact with several of his fellow student graduates to work in a Black community for 4-5 years after graduation to give their talents and skills in service where they were needed. It is not inconceivable that Professor Redmond influenced the group in their decision, as he is a man of great Black pride and an associate member of the Black Arts Movement (BAM) still underway in Harlem, with a kindred friendship to BAM founder Amiri Baraka (formerly known as LeRoi Jones).

Upon arriving in Harlem, New York, Michael would meet Barbara Ann Teer (11 years his senior) and they would fall in love. (Encounter #2) Michael shared his experience meeting Miles Davis shortly after he began dating Barbara Ann:

> "...I was shocked to receive a call from the famous trumpeter Miles Davis asking me to have drinks with him. When I arrived, I remember him looking me up and down then finally saying "I just wanted to know who this nigga is that Barbara picked over me!" (Encounter #3)

Being fresh out of college, Michael was unemployed. Barbara Ann called her friend Reginald Petty and asked him to give Michael a job. Reg reviewed Michael's background, which was quite interesting. His father, George I. Lythcott, worked for the National Institute of Health (NIH) in Ghana, with Prime Minister and President Kwame Nkrumah. The family moved from Shawnee, Oklahoma to Ghana in 1962. Michael would attend boarding schools in Ghana and Kenya. Michael originally wanted to join the seminary in Oklahoma and become a priest. Regism – "spirituality draws spirituality." Michael was fluent in several languages. Reg interviewed him and immediately hired him. He gave Michael one week's salary before he started work so that he could buy clothing, etc.

Michael recalled that Reg put together a new and eclectic training staff, comprised of grass roots black folks without college degrees but who knew how to navigate the communities. Michael's first assignment was a 6-8-week training cycle in the US Virgin Islands before releasing the trainees into their community jobs. There was an issue, though. The vendors at Charlotte Amalie, Virgin Islands, said that they had not been paid. Within two weeks of working, Reg wanted him to go to the V.I. and address what was happening. Michael was in shock! He felt that he was being naïve and wondered if Reg was setting him up for failure. He begrudgingly complied with the request. Michael figured out what was wrong and how the puzzle should be fixed. Reg wired the funds to Charlotte Amalie, US Virgin Islands, and Michael disbursed them. It was a great win for Michael and really molded and changed his life! He came to realize that Reg had a good feeling for people and knew what Michael was capable of doing. He stated that Reg was incredibly supportive of him and overall encouraging. Michael stated he never had a boss as smart and nurturing as Reg through the tenure of his working life.

Michael would be assigned to help adapt the Peace Corps cultural training component for VISTA volunteers, particularly in the America Pacific properties which expanded to Puerto Rico. Michael was in his early 20's and was the Director of Training in the Virgin Islands. He trained young people from Oklahoma and Nevada but there was a high incidence of early termination with the trainees – they could not do the job. Michael noticed that there was no cross-cultural or intercultural training. He told this to Reg and Reg's reply was "Write one!"

Fred Margolis was head of a learner centered training group and his was the latest method. The headquarters of VISTA was in the same building as Peace Corps. A global cross-cultural training curriculum needed to be written. Reg's philosophy was for teaching people how to care for themselves instead of being cared for. With volunteers quitting and not leaving notes on actions/progress made, this was a disaster. Per Reg, "A taste of honey is better than no taste at all." Michael would go on to describe Reg's philosophy as **Productive Confidence**. Michael was now on a hand-selected team to address this need for documentation for the Peace Corps. He viewed this as a teachable moment to create a training design. He would meet and work with David Levine on this project – entering within the circle of Reg influencers. Michael stated that his experience not only changed his life but the lives of people all over the world. He humbly and tearfully remarked to me that:

> "Reg never wanted the credit or the glory. He never grabbed the microphone but always wanted to see his protégés shine. If lost in the ocean, Reg would be the life vest. You would always be able to float."

Years later, while Reg was the Peace Corps Director in Swaziland, Michael worked as the Peace Corps Training Director in Botswana while wearing a red, black, and green cap. Michael also did a research project in

Swaziland with Reg. Michael would ultimately go from the Peace Corps to the US State Department.

Michael learned a great deal at the feet of Reg Petty, including how to begin the conversation when speaking to an outsider coming into a community to work:

> "…Go to the people, listen to them, understand what they know and understand. Build your plan on what they already know and understand. Then they will turn to each other and say "Look what we have done for ourselves" …"

Per Michael, this allowed the people to own the work. "Reg created a sense of independence and pride in the people he worked with." He gave the example from Reg of a time when building a new office in one of the African countries. The builders wanted to build a sidewalk. Reg told them not to build the sidewalk. *"Don't create the path. Open the building and let the building operate for a month. Then look at the grass and see where they stepped. Then you can build the sidewalk."*

Michael views Reg as a very humble man and all the higher ups noticed him. Everywhere he went, magic happened. He could have been a millionaire many times over, but he chose to remain in the background. He relayed four tenets of Reg's success, in his eyes:

> "1. He has a good eye for talent.
>
> 2. He is adept at selecting the right person for the right job.
>
> 3. He communicates a crystal-clear vision.
>
> 4. He gives you the resources you need to bring actions to fruition."

"Reg is not standing by you; he is sitting in the stands and smiling". Michael refers to Reg as a "Selfless Magician".

Barbara Ann would travel internationally as a dancer. In 1968, she would create and open the National Black Theatre in Harlem, New York. This project grew from her disillusionment with the negative stereotypes and limited acting roles offered to black women. Over the next five decades, she would develop a groundbreaking methodology available exclusively at her theatre called **TEER – The Technology of Soul**. She would continue her travels to Africa during this time, in part on a fellowship from the Coca Cola Foundation, with one of its Board of Directors members being Donald McHenry, an East St. Louis native who would go on to become the 15th United States Ambassador to the United Nations and is a lifelong friend and confidant of Reginald Petty. (Encounter #4) Michael and Barbara Ann would have two children, Michael F. Lythcott, a successful serial entrepreneur, and Barbara A. "Sade" Lythcott, who currently is the CEO of the National Black Theatre.

When working with Reginald Petty, he is adept at testing you for your knowledge. He does not suffer fools as that is a waste of his time. Michael remarked that Reg's mantra is "Show me what you're working with." I know that to be true as Reg employed that philosophy with me while interviewing me to write this book. I thank God, my parents, my family, and educators for preparing me to make the grade with Reg.

Reg would spend several years in Washington, DC, affectionately known as "Chocolate City", in the early to mid-1970s. Black people dominated the local politics of the city, with its first mayor being Walter Washington, who served as the first and only Mayor-Commissioner from 1967-1974, and the first home-rule mayor from 1975-1979. Reg would become great friends with the next and two-time mayor of DC, Marion Barry. Reg was quite impressed with his friend's life story, including earning the rank of Eagle Scout with the Boy Scouts of America at age 17, participating in sit-ins in Nashville to desegregate lunch counters during graduate studies in organic chemistry at Fisk University, and working on his doctoral degree in Chemistry at the University of Tennessee in Knoxville. Mayor Barry was also a civil rights activist who served as the first chairman of SNCC. Their membership in SNCC was a blood bond between the two men. Another bonding organization would be Pride, Incorporated, a Department of Labor funded program co-founded by

Barry with his future wife, Mary Treadwell, which advocated for poor youth and helped them find employment.

Reg would also become friends with Anthony Williams, a finance guy who would later become Mayor of DC. Reg believed that they brought in good people but there was little to no accountability. He also felt that Barry's vision was larger than Washington, DC. At this time, folks like Walter Fauntroy, Delano 'Del' Lewis, and Eleanor Holmes Norton were in political offices. Reg was not involved in DC politics but supported his friends. He did bid on small city improvement activities.

## Another Political Appointment

Reg would be appointed as the Director of Research for the National Advisory Council on Vocational Education (NACVE) by President Gerald Ford in 1974. In this appointment, Reg was in Washington, DC and had to work in a more in-your-face politically driven environment. Reg ultimately became Executive Director of NACVE. He routinely worked with Congress and made reports to high-ranking political figures on the state of vocational education in the United States. It was critically important to him that minorities benefit from this appointment, ensuring that at least 20% of support went to African Americans and the handicapped. Congresswoman Shirley Chisholm, who also had the distinction of being named the Secretary of the House Democratic Caucus during the 95th and 96th Congress, helped him draft the documentation used during his post.

Reg was already adept at "playing the game" when it came to political situations and was committed to providing the same no nonsense and savvy support to the youth in the program as he did in his other political appointments. He worked cooperatively with his team and colleagues and found this one of the most gratifying positions he held. He came full circle from starting one of the first Job Corps centers in America to running the entire VocEd national program! This brother from East St. Louis, Illinois, was representing his city well.

## Reg...The Author

Reg never stopped developing ways to create career education opportunities for minorities in America. Published in 1973, Reg, along with Larry Davenport, wrote a book entitled *Minorities and Career Education*. Reg was working as the Director of Research for the NACVE in Washington, D.C. Larry was the Chairman of the NACVE. In the book, Larry and Reg define career education as "...designed to prepare students for the attaché case professions as well as the lunch box occupations...to give every youngster a genuine choice, as well as the intellectual and occupational skills necessary to back it up..."

The book touches on numerous topics penned by multiple authoritative sources which are especially relevant today, including:

- Public Schools, Public Policy, Public Problems: Some Observations and Suggestions;
- Career Education: A Tool for the Minority Veteran;
- Winners and Losers in the Good Life Contest: Implications of Career Education on Poor Youth;
- Career Education and the Community College;
- Counselors, Career Education and Minorities,
- and Career Education, Professional Preparation and Minority Groups

One of the most fascinating chapters to me was *Career Education for Women: The Feminist Movement in Career Education.* The sub-topics addressed sexual role definitions in career education *stemming from* early home conditioning in sex roles, and how these attitudes are *perpetrated* throughout elementary, secondary and college learning for women. The revelations and common-sense approaches to meeting the goals of the book are a must read for anyone who cares about the education of children in America.

Meeting with Petty, U.S. Government Officials, and East St. Louis City Government and Civic leaders.

Seated: Unknown man; Dr. Fred Kimbrough, Assistant Secretary of Education; Mayor James Williams; Assistant Secretary of Labor; Fred Teer. Standing: Reginald Petty, Director National Advisory Council on Vocational Education; Dr. Grice, SIUE; Unnamed; Unnamed; Dr. William Mason, Superintendent of School District 189; Unnamed; Gordon Bush, Council member; Dr. Roosevelt Johnson. Photo from Petty archives.

Burkina Faso Director of Cattle, Petty (Peace Corps Country Director), and the Deputy Director of Agriculture. Photo from Petty archives.

Petty (Peace Corps Country Director in Burkina Faso) with unnamed country officials. Photo from Petty archives.

Petty and then Vice President of Burkina Faso.
Photo from Petty archives.

Peace Corps Country Director Petty with Peace Corps Volunteers Kathy Brinn, Paul Alagana, and Dana Mitchell. Photo from Petty archives.

Petty and Lucy at Victoria Falls Waterfall in Zimbabwe. Photo from Petty archives.

Petty and Lucy - a Night on the Town. Photo from Petty archives.

Petty, Lucy and Tom Fox with Peace Corps Volunteers and their families. Photo from Petty archives.

Petty with Kenyan President and Peace Corps Volunteers at a social function. Photo from Petty archives.

Petty with African delegation. Photo from Petty archives.

Peace Corps Country Director Petty meeting with Peace Corps Volunteers. Photo from Petty archives.

Petty with Peace Corps volunteers and residents. Photo from Petty archives.

*The Pandemic Prophet*

Petty with African delegation. Photo from Petty archives.

Bruce Sr. and Helen Petty at anniversary party. Photo from Petty archives.

Bruce Sr. and Helen Petty at home. Photo from Petty archives.

Candid photo of Petty. Photo from Petty archives.

Jaye P. Willis

## How Ungrateful
### By Reginald Petty

After all we have done for them
We gave them food when they were hungry
We send them medical supplies
We sent missionaries
We taught them the American way
It's not our fault they wouldn't listen
All we wanted was their natural resources
And human labor
After all, that's the way the market operates
HOW UNGRATEFUL

# THREE SCORE

# Swaziland to Swagger-land

**(41-60) 1976-1995**

**Phenom Prince**

(a kwansaba tribute poem)

*Fused with Crispus Attucks courage, this Polack
town Prince inhaled culture, style, and pride
from the East Side, lappin' up Champaign and
Carbon'd-ale knoll-edge, stoutly strivin' for
civil Job et Peace Corps D'Afrique by
way of Burkina Faso through Swaziland via
Seychelles to Boogie origin, droppin' learned swagger.*

By Jaye P. Willis

As America was preparing to celebrate its 200th birthday, Reg was preparing for the next chapter in his life. Reg was leaving his position as the Executive Director National Advisory Council on Vocational Education and the Presidential Advisory Council for which he served from 1972-1976 to begin a second tour as a Peace Corps Country Director in Africa. An appreciation dinner was given for Reg in Washington, DC, which his family attended in full force. Parents Bruce Sr. and Helen, wife Lucy, children Tony, Joel, Amina, brother Bruce and wife Madeline.

The night was captured photographically by Reg's dear friend Roland L. Freeman. An award-winning photo documentarian, Freeman co-directed the Mississippi FolkLife Project for the Smithsonian Institution's Center for Folklife and Cultural Heritage in 1970, among many other historic undertakings. One of his books, *Margaret Walker's "For My People": A Tribute* (1992) was given to me by Reg to read and study for this book. As you can imagine, the photographs are amazing and the prose transformative. Freeman's photographs of the appreciation dinner for Reg are captured in black and white, adding a richness and nostalgia to the images. Presentations from friends, family, and elected officials rounded out the night. His dear friend, Marion Barry was in attendance as a member of the Council for the District of Columbia (a few years before becoming the Mayor of Washington, DC).

*The Pandemic Prophet*

Petty with friend Mayor Marion Barry

*Jaye P. Willis*

## **Encounters with a Black Panther**

Reg and Fredericka Teer (sister of Barbara Teer), both from East St. Louis, Illinois, shared a very special friend – Mr. Eldridge Cleaver, a leader in the Black Panther Party organization prominent in the United States from 1966 – 1976.

The former Black Panther knew that he was facing charges of attempted murder after an April 6, 1968 confrontation with Oakland Police resultant from the assassination of the Reverend Dr. Martin Luther King, Jr. two days earlier. No police officers were killed in the incident, but fellow Panther Bobby Hutton did lose his life.

Eldridge was a fugitive in the States, having fled America after jumping bail for the attempted murder charges. His first stop was Cuba. Reg had previously accompanied Eldridge to Cuba in the early 1960's to meet with Fidel Castro on the state of Black people in America. Travelling to Cuba in the 1960's had been banned for Americans, particularly after the Bay of Pigs invasion in 1961. According to Reg, the Black Power Movement had access to planes and boats from their association to the Mafia out of New York. Cleaver would go on to live in exile in Algeria in Northern Africa, and later in Paris, France.

Reg shared a copy of a letter that Eldridge wrote to Fredericka on June 1, 1972. The content was desperate and conspiratorial in nature. Eldridge believed that his life was in danger in Algiers, the capital of Algeria, and that he needed several thousands of dollars to flee the country before it was too late. Several compatriots were also abroad and seeking a return to the United States, including Joju, Sekou, Larry, D.C., Barbara, along with Pete and Charlotte and their child Malcolm. He indicates concerns from Nixon, Chou-En Lai, Huey, and billion-dollar oil contracts. He cited Reg in the letter several times as someone who would be pivotal in helping to raise the funds that he needed to flee Algeria.

Reg also shared a copy of a letter he received from Kathleen Neal Cleaver, wife of Eldridge, requesting funds to help him come back home to the United States from Africa. Eldridge and his wife were now in Senegal. On March 8, 1976, East St. Louis natives Fredricka Teer and Reg Petty worked with friend David Levine on efforts to raise bail for the Fair Trial for Eldridge Cleaver Fund. Reg wrote an impassioned declaration entitled "Notes on the Problem of EC", detailing Cleaver's alleged threats to democracy, his character assassination by the United States government, and the violation of his rights as an American citizen to espouse his political views.

Once Cleaver returned for trial, the charges were reduced to assault and Cleaver received a sentence of community service. Reg has maintained these letters over the years. They are especially important to him and a source of pride for the work he has done over his life – to right wrongs against those retaliated against for their principles.

## A Substantive Encounter

Before leaving the States, he would meet another branch of the REP Tree of Life. His name is Jack Healy. For those unfamiliar with this name, he is a treasure all to himself and worthy of research. To whet your appetite, Jack would become the Executive Director of Amnesty International.

Jack first met Reg in 1976 in St. Louis, Missouri while Jack served as an advance man for Dick Gregory (oh, that name). Jack had brought Dick to St. Louis with Muhammad Ali on April 23, 1976, providing publicity and fundraising for a special event. As Dick had come home, he contacted his lifelong friend Reg. Jack had previously heard about Reg for his efforts in Mississippi in the Civil Rights Movement. Turns out they were in the same areas about the same time working on voter registration drives but had not met each other. Jack's first impression of Reg was his physical appearance. He stood tall and confident. He knew that they would be friends for life after their first conversation. Jack described Reg as "Big, Strong, Cocky and Smart!"

Petty with Edna and dear friend Dick Gregory. Photo from Petty archives.

Jack worked with Reg again in the United States Peace Corps. Jack was the Peace Corps Country Director in Lesotho, Africa. He lived next door to Chris Hani of the African National Congress, who was assassinated in 1993. Jack described Chris as a fierce opponent of apartheid and a brilliant military leader.

Norman Rush was Peace Corps Country Director in Botswana, Africa and Reg was Peace Corps Country Director in Swaziland. These three worked together and trained Peace Corps volunteers in Southern Africa. They discouraged White volunteers from going to Pretoria on weekends and vacations as their Black counterparts could not go there. The trio of Country Directors met in Pretoria and Johannesburg, South Africa regularly. Jack and Norman are White, and of course, Reg is Black.

Jack shared a story involving the three Country Directors:

> "On one particular occasion in 1979, the trio of Directors and the recruits met at the Intercontinental Hotel in Johannesburg, South Africa for a dance. The Blacks and Whites danced together. The police stopped them due to mixed races dancing together. The police had a hotline to Pretoria, the capitol

of South Africa. They were told they could keep dancing but only until 2:00 am." Jack found it funny that apartheid took a break for the dance.

Jack described Reg as the spiritual leader of the trio. Reg created newsletters and other documents for the Country Directors. David Levine, then Director of Peace Corps' Office of Programming and Training Coordination in Washington, D.C., was an incredibly good friend of the trio as well. Jack recalls that David was very protective of Reg and that Reg would contact David for anything that the group needed. Jack recalls the trio of himself, Norman, and Reg to be quite the triple threat, as they were called in and grilled by the United States Congress regularly. The Congressional concerns stemmed from the close proximity of these Country Directors to many African leaders who defiantly opposed apartheid and were supposed members of the Communist party. They feared the trio's apparent relationships with these leaders and many in Congress believed that they held the same views, which were at the time opposite of the United States views on apartheid and communism. Jack stated that South Carolina Senator Jesse Helms often complained about what they were doing as Country Directors in the South African region and accused them of hiring communists to assist them in their duties. Each of the trio vowed that if one were fired, the others would resign in solidarity.

To emphasize this, Jack told the story of when he hired a Black Lesotho nurse to work with him. When he returned from a trip, he found that the nurse had been fired. When he asked why, he was told that she was militant and combative, along with her husband. Jack did not believe this and investigated the allegations. He found them to be false, as he expected.

Per Jack, Reg engineered all the civil rights issues for the trio. Jack described Norman as the quiet activist, David was the politically savvy and diplomatic player, and himself as the anarchist. He lovingly referred to Reg as the heart and soul of the group, leading them in all civil rights and civil disobedience efforts.

## Growing up Petty (Joel and Amina)

Joel and Amina were born in Washington, DC prior to Reg's Peace Corps term. Joel is the elder of the two. Lucy recalled that Reg never denied his children, even though Joel was born "perfectly white". Both Joel and Amina are very fair skinned.

Joel and Amina Petty. Photo from Petty archives.

Amina is the quintessential Daddy's Girl. Her entire conversation with me regarding her Dad was notes of music and joy. I could feel her smiling through the phone. Amina encapsulated her experience of living abroad in endearing terms.

> "I remember moving to Africa when I was seven and staying there until about the age of 12. I recall traveling a lot and feeling that my Dad was very important. We also went to a lot of parties. My experience was mostly in Swaziland and Kenya. In Swaziland, we had a lot of little stone figurines, about an inch tall, which looked like monster finger puppets. Joel and I played with them all the time but were supposed to place them back on the shelf because they were not

toys. My Dad had several chess sets. We used to make up games with the chess pieces like armies, cities, etc. They were made of different materials like brass and ivory."

As a child, Amina remembered her Dad as calming, mellow and soft spoken and not surrounding himself with a lot of controversy. The exposure of being raised abroad at such a young age left an indelible imprint on her spirit as she experienced and saw things many people did not see. From her young perspective, all was perfect. She cannot even recall a time when her parents argued.

Life in Swaziland was not without excitement, especially for a young girl who looked White. Amina remembers traveling to South Africa with her parents and brother and not fully understanding why folks looked at her parents differently. She did note that she felt outraged by the treatment they received. She spoke of a huge picture of her parents on the front page of a newspaper because they were at a party in Johannesburg. They were not being treated as diplomats but as some sort of unnatural anomaly. People would approach her Mom asking if she was 'okay' while walking with her children and husband. This was a heavy load for a young girl to bear, especially when her circumstance was 'normal' in her eyes and mind.

Amina further recalled that crossing the boarder from Swaziland to South Africa was extremely dangerous because of the roadblocks, folks with machine guns, soldiers, hummers and having to wait for hours to move. She shared one very strange and funny story with me from her time in South Africa.

"My family and I were in either Johannesburg or Durban walking down the street when a Black African man approached my Mom asking her if he could talk to my Dad about buying me for his wife, even promising to throw in a few cows! I was nine years old at the time. The bartering of people was really strange to me."

The family left Swaziland for their new home in Kenya, her Dad's next assignment. This was around 1981. Amina described a daily routine of waking up in the morning with the radio on in the house. One day the news was on and she remembers her Mom and the cook in the house. A coup was taking place in Kenya and Amina could hear gunshots all around the property. She was told that she could not go outside. She was about 10 or 11 at the time but recalls that she was not too afraid because she knew what a coup was, and she felt secure because her parents told her everything was okay. Reg and Lucy imparted a level of life lessons and knowledge within their children that was far in advance of their ages which not only kept them safe but kept their minds and spirits agile. The family returned to Washington, DC in the 1980's, or as Amina put it "…leaving the paradise of Africa and moving to DC." In her perspective, what she saw in Africa prepared her to live in DC and not be so traumatized. I found that sentiment remarkably interesting.

Joel fondly remembered living overseas. He believes that it is good to see and live different ideologies for intellectual and spiritual growth. He recalled playing rugby while in Swaziland and Kenya. He also attended British schools which were extremely strict. He was told to speak proper English both at the schools and when he returned to the states, particularly when at home in East St. Louis. He was diagnosed as dyslexic while in the British schools which made learning without the proper assistance and tools more difficult.

Joel was 13 years old when they returned to Washington, DC. The look then was tight jeans and a large afro, which he happily donned. He remembers his parents having to sue the city to get him in the proper school to address his dyslexia. They won the suit, and he attended the Chelsea private school, with the tuition being paid for by the city.

Amina clearly remembered people always saying to her "I love your Dad!" She remembers a time when her paternal grandmother sent her a letter about him, including report cards and other miscellaneous items, so that she could better understand and know this man. Amina stated "…He has a calming effect on people. He listens, always listening, giving them his complete attention." Even in separate interviews, Joel echoes the sentiment that Reg was a very good listener.

When their parents divorced, neither child was shocked, but both stated they did not see the divorce coming. Joel went on further to say that he was not angry. They never argued in front of them, but Amina could tell when her Mother was mad by the look on her face (a trait that she shares with her). She came to know that there were bitter feelings between them, but they handled it like adults. She was just leaving college when it happened, as they decided to wait until the children were adults before unraveling the familial stable foundation. Joel moved out of the house when his parents divorced and started his "grown up" life. They wanted their children to succeed without the excuses or pressure that comes with divorce.

Joel knew Reg to be very direct in his manner and encouraged him to be the same. He never told Joel what to do but that he had to figure out what he wanted and then do it. Joel wanted to be the first Black governor of Illinois. Reg shared his ideology with him: "**You must allow yourself to be entitled to be great.**"

Reg always demanded respect from everyone, especially his children. Joel recalled one day, as a young adult, he was verbally disrespecting his father. Reg struck him, knocking him into the fireplace. He knew that respect was the bedrock of Reg's foundation. He never disrespected him again.

In Joel's eyes, Reg is a "quiet hero" who lives by his core values. He believes that his Dad could have been wealthy by owning stock in Coca-Cola, IBM, and other companies, but Reg does not value wealth or notoriety. Reg values service to his fellow man, education, and the development of talent/self-worth in others. He realizes that the world will only improve if everyone has the opportunity to give their best. ***But that cannot happen with the socio-economic mores of racial superiority, untethered capitalism, and suppression of education for the non-elite.*** Joel lived in East St. Louis while attending State Community College. The city has its dangerous spots, like any other city, and Joel was stabbed twice while someone was trying to steal his bike. He lived with his brother Tony (10 years older) in St. Louis for six or seven years. Tony is a very gifted musician and Joel loves music. Tony provided a less restrictive lifestyle for Joel.

Joel recalls being afraid of his paternal grandmother, Helen. He remembers taking piano lessons from her. Tony and Joel would ask "why is Grandma so old-fashioned?" She was strict and demanding, not just on Reg but on all her family.

Joel's ex-wife is a Navajo Indian. Their son, Elijah, is of mixed ethnicity – Black, White, and Native American. Joel followed the Unitarian religion while living in Carlinville, Illinois with his maternal grandparents. He quips "Be careful with religion and who you take it away from!" In his estimation, his family is either really Black or really White. Joel is currently engaged to a lovely African American woman named Cher. They have three cats – Wednesday, Pugsley, and Peanut. Joel's overall view of his Dad is simple – **He is gentle, which compliments his physical stature, and he has a sense of purpose.** I echo those sentiments.

Her parents' issues never affected Amina but impacted her relationship with men. Her Dad was gone a lot. She understands both sides of what they went through and stated, "No one has a right to judge." Her Mom would remarry and enjoyed a good relationship for many years until her second husband's death from a heart attack. Reg would remarry as well, to Edna Patterson, a local artist and art therapist from East St. Louis. Amina was fine with that match as they complement each other and do so much to support one another. She believes that he is the type of man that needs to be with someone. Edna and Reg's marriage would last longer than her parents.

Amina and Edna are more alike. Amina confided that she has an anxiety disorder and that makes her uncomfortable around a lot of people. This feeling extends to her relationship with her brother Tony, who is very much like her. She loves him but he is also introverted, and they don't communicate well, not talking very often. She adds though that when they do talk, it is great. Amina has a son in the Navy in Great Lakes, Illinois and a daughter in Brooklyn, New York. She also has a teenage son living at home with her. They adore Reg and plan to visit with him soon.

Amina's perception of her Dad echoes Joel's. Her Dad lives by his morals and practices what he preaches. He is very willing to admit his faults and does not down others for their mistakes. She, too, believes that he deserves more accolades that he has received. Her Dad will never bore you when he tells a story. She stressed to me to complete this book. In truth, Amina is my muse as she opened her soul to me and let me witness her Dad through her. She shared two stories with me that encapsulate Reg, the man.

> "One day, Dad was walking through Central Park and somehow lost all his money. This guy then tried to rob him. Dad told the guy to "Go fuck yourself" in strong terms. The guy was confused and did not pursue the robbery, saying "Man, I was trying to rob you!" as he fled.
>
> I also remember going to an event with Dad which Jesse Jackson was attending. Mr. Jackson had that glazed look that famous people have when shaking hands with people. The he looked at my Dad and his attitude changed. He was elated and asked Dad how he was doing. I remember him being genuinely happy to see him. I smiled and said, "That's my Dad!"

## A Substantive Encounter Too

Hank Collins looks back fondly on his one encounter with Reginald Petty. They only met one time, but the impact was substantial.

After Hank graduated from Humboldt State University in California, he joined the United States Peace Corps. He was assigned to the African country of Kenya (September 1979 – December 1981).

While working in Kenya, he lived in a village where only one person had a vehicle. For him to get to town, he had to try to catch a ride on a truck that went between the village and the town (Nairobi) once per week, which was also frequently delayed. At the time, he had a Country Director who was not a fan of his. To address his travel concerns between the town and the village, he purchased a motorcycle from one of the volunteers who was leaving. Now, The Country Director let some of the volunteers have motorcycles but not all. When Hank acquired his motorcycle, the Country Director threatened to have him kicked out of the Peace Corps.

Hank was not going to be kicked out without a fight. He contacted his school officials and the Peace Corps to complain about his treatment and his desire to remain as a volunteer.

At the same time, the Country Director was being replaced with a new Country Director, Reginald Petty. Hank believes that Mr. Petty received his letter and contacted him, stating that it made no sense to kick him out of the Corps over a motorcycle and that he could remain and finish out his time. Mr. Petty even went so far as to tell him "…he wanted to fly me back to the States to meet the President because I had the balls to get the motorcycle…" Recalling this fond memory made Hank laugh.

When he left the Peace Corps, Hank attended medical school, first in Grenada but had to leave after the country had a coup, then finishing at Northwestern University in Illinois – the home state of Reginald Petty!

Dr. Hank Collins currently practices medicine in California. He remarked to Reg in a recent conversation "You saved my life. Thank you for being there for me." Being able to list service in the Peace Corps on a resume is a great accomplishment and favorably viewed by prospective employers. To be dishonorably discharged from this service carries blight on your record. Fortunately, the latter did not happen for Dr. Collins and allowed him to pursue his dream of becoming a physician.

Reg's Presidential appointments stemmed from his academic prowess and outstanding successes working with vocational education and Peace Corps assignments. In addition to his Peace Corps appointments by John F. Kennedy and Lyndon Johnson, he was also appointed by Gerald Ford to serve on US National Advisory Council for Vocational Education (NACVE), as well as Jimmy Carter on both NACVE and Peace Corps Country Director for Swaziland, continuing to Kenya and the Seychelles.

## The Ultimate Encounter

Reg often found himself in Johannesburg to perform the required duties of Peace Corps Director of Swaziland. On a normal day in 1991, as Reg was walking down the street, he ran into a familiar face coming towards him. It was John H. Hicks, another brother from East St. Louis, Illinois! When Reg and John saw each other, they both burst into laughter. Reg recalled saying "Man, no one is ever going to believe this! I would say let's get a cup of coffee but there is no place we can enter!" Remember, the practice of apartheid was just ending in South Africa.

John had the distinction of being the first Black reporter for the St. Louis Post Dispatch Newspaper. He later became a foreign service officer for the United States Information Agency (USIA). He also held State Department posts in Liberia Africa, Berlin Germany, Greece and Washington, DC. He was then named cultural attaché in the United States Embassy in South Africa.

## Back in the USA (again)

Reg returned to the United States after completion of his Peace Corps tours in Kenya and the Seychelles. He went back to Washington, DC where he again rekindled his work relationship with David Levine. His views on character and respect had been broadened by his work overseas. Reg's lack of tolerance for rude behavior was a particular character trait of his. Lucy recalled a time when the family was on a bus in the 1980's. Some young people were playing a boom box loudly and annoying the passengers. Several older folks on the bus asked them to lower the music but the youth refused. Reg took the boom box and threw it out the window! He did not believe in using profanity around the children. She likened Reg to a politician, further stating that he understands boundaries but refuses to live in a box. It is actions like this and others that Reg and his friends have relayed to me that brought me to the conclusion that Reg lived his life as a martyr, even inviting death at some instances, but the grim reaper was not ready for him. That preclusion is a happy gift to us and the world.

*Jaye P. Willis*

# The African Development Foundation

The development of the African Development Foundation (ADF) was signed into law in 1980 during the Carter administration. Its overall goal was to attempt to counter some of the limitations faced by official development assistance programs such as those of the World Bank and the United States Agency for International Development (USAID). Though started during the Carter administration, it was subsequently stalled for several years due to delays with the appointment of the Board of Directors and later an unexpected turnover of top staff which resulted in a General Accounting Office (GAO) audit of managerial capacity. The organization was ready to stand-up in 1984 with the appointment of a president and vice-president of the organization. Constance Hilliard and Reginald Petty were appointed to those roles, respectively.

Unfortunately, there were major disagreements on how to proceed with funding for the affected African nations among other issues which resulted in both Ms. Hilliard and Reg resigning their posts within a few months of their appointments. Reg recalls that the discussions that he had with lawmakers when he agreed to take on this post were not adhered to, as well as other issues regarding some board members who had little to no working knowledge of dealing with African countries or their politics. He viewed these obstacles as detrimental to the goals of the organization and the peoples it would serve. As a man of strong principle, he resigned his post but continued to serve as an advisor to the new leadership. With Reg's Peace Corps and consulting experience in numerous African nations, he was well positioned to assist in this manner.

## *Dropping Knowledge*

Reg was a sought-after speaker for colleges and universities, particularly on the East Coast. Below is an address that he presented at the University of Pennsylvania in 1988. On the original document, his hand-written title, "There is Enough for Everyone's Needs" is derived from a quote from legendary nonviolent resistance leader Mahatma Gandhi. This is a sample of the treasure trove of truths in his residential archive.

## There is Enough for Everyone's Needs

Each generation has a responsibility to improve the quality of life on this planet. While at 53 years of age, I am far from finished as a change agent; I feel it is my duty to begin to pass to you the experiences, good and bad, which have formed my American generation's attitudes toward other people of the world. Let me say that we seem not to learn much from the experience of others, whether they be individual or group. The number of wars that we have had and continue to have on this planet is proof enough of this statement. The poverty that exists, even in countries of plenty, adds additional testimony.

In the next 15-20 minutes, I will attempt to provide you with a framework within which my generation can begin to pass the development torch—the torch of progress—to your generation. History suggests that the 1960's was the time of greatest concern for international developmental issues.

It was the time of personal activism, of Peace Corps, VISTA in the U.S., and many of your organizations, such as CUSA, were, I believe, founded during this period. Young people were concerned and active in raising environmental issues. We questioned the assumption that poverty and famine would always be with us and there was nothing that we could do. We questioned the morality of the political models which resulted in a few controlling and benefitting from the majority of the world's resources. We regarded racism, whether at home or abroad, as anathema to civilized society. We traveled around the world to help others and to bring a message of hope. At home we were quite a nuisance to those in power: we raised questions about their goals, objectives, and methods, we interjected humanism in places that those in power felt it did not belong, such as in economic and political decision making.

We wondered why products could not be developed that were useful to humanity and safe to the environment. During this time, many organizations were formed whose goal was to serve as watchdogs of the corporations. People came together to form businesses and seek out alternative ways of production. The idea that "more is better" was questioned and many people tried to simplify their lives by creating so-called alternative lifestyles. There was a back to the land movement among many young people, and groups came together, even in urban areas, to share scarce resources and assist each other in child rearing and income production. Cooperatives of all kinds sprang up all over North America, Europe, South America, and Africa. Certainly, in South America and Africa, these were not new; but during the 1960's, in the U.S., Europe, and other "developed" countries, an appreciation and recognition of cooperatives surfaced. Hence, funding, and other resources were made available to enhance their development.

Altruism was in the air – J.F. Kennedy said: "Ask not what your country can do for you, but what you can do for your country." Volunteerism was in vogue and change was in the air. Experimentation was the order of the day, and movements of all kinds sprang up. For change agents this was nirvana. The great society was just around the corner. We thought that we would see an end to poverty and racism in our generation. Well strange things happened on the way to this "perfect society"; J.F. Kennedy, Bobby Kennedy and Reverend Martin Luther King were assassinated within a few years of each other. Nixon was elected president of the United States:

we found out that we as youth of that period had little staying power or understanding of the change process—we did not understand the psychological, economic, and political commitments that a people build up over time and how threatening change is to most people. Especially when the future is clouded with abstractions or peace and equality, but short of specifics of how this newfound society will impact on their jobs, social standing, religious and political values.

For many, and probably most Americans, things were moving too fast. The picture of "hippies" on television each evening railing against the system, both verbally and in their attire (long hair and beads), were seen by many conservative elements of society as not believing in the work ethic. Young people (flower children) on the corner asking for handouts and descriptions of the drug scene in sections of our cities (which was considered by many as a part of the rebellion) was a bit more than middle America could take, and hence the retreat to safer grounds. Nixon promised that we could go back to old values, and we did—and Watergate followed.

We must not feel, however, that the movements bred in the 1960s were a total loss: nothing could be further from the truth. U.S. relationships with economically depressed countries were changed drastically. No longer do we simply impose wide ranging developmental schemes on a nation without at least that country's leadership knowledgeable of and/or in agreement with the scheme. This does not necessarily mean that success is guaranteed, but it is certainly enhanced. The existence of so many former Peace Corps volunteers in development organizations who speak local languages bring a reality to the developmental process which had not existed previously. The insistence on grassroots development is a direct result of the influence of these former grassroots volunteers, who are now in leadership positions in these developmental organizations. There are many other examples that one could draw upon to illustrate the positive impact of the 1960s on today's decision makers.

Well, what does all of this have to do with Third World development today and what does it have to do with you? Hopefully, a great deal.

When we look at the Third World, we see most of the world's natural resources, including timber reserves, oil, coal, diamonds, platinum, uranium, soil, etc. However, despite this natural wealth, most of these resources are controlled by countries of the western world. There are historical reasons for this which I am sure you are aware of, however, what impact does this history of exploitation have on us today? Let me note a few examples which may serve to place in proper perspective the relationship between the developed and underdeveloped countries, sometimes referred to as the Third World.

In the underdeveloped world:

1. 40,000 young children die each day from diseases which could be prevented.
2. 100,000,000 children go to bed hungry each night.
3. 40% of the world's children lack safe water to drink and adequate medical care
4. In Latin America, 40 million children depend on street earnings to sustain themselves and their families.
5. One person in four is without decent housing or has none at all.

At the same time in one day in the U.S.:

- Americans spend $700 million or more than $8,000 each second on entertainment and recreation, which is about what is spent on national defense.
- Americans spend $300 million on clothes.
- Americans buy 38,000 of Barbie and Ken dolls and 55,000 pieces of doll clothing which makes Mattel Corporation one of the leading manufacturers of women's clothing.
- The amount given by the U.S. to aid economic development in other nations is two-tenths of 1% of the total gross national product—the least given by any of the 17 leading economic powers that are members of the aid committee of the Organization of Economic Development (OED).

-New York Times, 1986

Another way of looking at the problem is that **in a world spending $800 billion a year on military programs, one adult in three cannot read and one in four is hungry.** Also, it costs $590,000 a day to operate an aircraft carrier, of which less than 1% would feed the 14,000 children who die in Africa each day from hunger or hunger related diseases.

**Can anything be done to alleviate the suffering that we see all around us if we but look?** Many say that hunger is the fault of the hungry or God's will. That there is not enough food to go around. Hunger is often used as a weapon to punish those who do not follow a particular philosophy or pattern of behavior. Many countries refuse to provide assistance to children in another country because that country does not support the former's policies. Do we really believe that the children know or care about these philosophical differences while they slowly starve to death?

Yes, hunger and poverty can be eliminated. Will it be easy? No!! Most critical is the will of Earth's population, and particularly those countries controlling the world's resources. My generation has been too concerned about its own comfort to give more than token assistance. Do not be deceived by the sporadic outpouring of assistance to specific famine victims who happen to reach the attention of the media (Ethiopia being an example). This support is short lived and ignores similar famine conditions in surrounding countries, e.g., Mozambique.

The hypocrisy of the rest, to me at times, is appalling. We make passionate speeches about human rights and get righteously indignant about individual cases of mistreatment of the Earth's young, but refuse to modify our behavior or give more than token gifts to truly bring about the changes in which we say we believe.

Gandhi stated: **"There is enough for everyone's needs, but not everyone's greed."**

Omar Bradley, an American general, stated: **"We have grasped the Mystery of the atom and rejected the Sermon on the Mount… We know more about war than we know about peace, more about killing than about living."**

My personal reason for coming before you is to ask that you continue a process begun by the rest of my generation during the best periods of their lives. I ask you to look at the planet on which you live and acknowledge the brotherhood and sisterhood of all its residents. I ask you not to accept poverty as a natural state of humankind. I ask you to internalize in your personal life the statement made by Gandhi.

I ask you to talk to your younger brothers and sisters and pledge to them that you will work to improve the quality of their lives.

I ask you to develop the staying power that was lacking in the majority of people of my generation – for change does not come quickly. I ask those of you from more affluent countries and families to reach out to those without your economic advantages and pledge them your assistance as they struggle to throw off their economic bondage. I ask you to learn to listen to the soul of humanity for only there will you find truth. I ask you to listen with modesty and care. I ask you to involve yourself in programs that will restructure the priorities of the Western nations to truly make them their brother's keeper.

I ask you to heed the concern of Dr. Martin Luther King: "**A nation that continues year after year to spend more on military defense than on programs of social uplift is approaching spiritual death.**"

You are probably familiar with the major issues of development. The Third World must produce more food, better housing, develop healthier populations, increase the educational level of its people, develop a healthier economy which produces job and employment opportunities for its people. It must decrease its population growth rate, involve women in all levels of activities as equals (we simply cannot substitute one form of discrimination for another), find methods of marketing its products which work to the advantage of the country's people (and not just a few multinational corporations), develop local capital which can then be used for internal growth without total dependence on international bankers. The Third World must find some way to get out of the credit crunch in which it now finds itself.

Presently, all or most of the "developing world's" surplus goes to pay off interest on loans made years ago, often by Presidents or Dictators long gone. It is my belief that any country is only as stable as its base. In most cases, agriculture forms this base.

We can live without many things, but food and water are basic; and hence must form the underpinning for any society. Unfortunately in many Third World countries – overgrazing, single crop cultivation, dependence on Western fertilizer, use of Western seeds, lack of water, and over population have led to many fleeing to the cities with accompanying problems. None of the problems are without solutions. In many cases, the solutions are rather simple in development terms, but are particularly not popular. For example, increasing the price of food raises the standard of living in rural areas, but generates complaints from urban residents. Politically, however, urban residents who are government employees, better educated and more tied to things, are the most likely to be politically active. Government officials tend to lean over backwards to support this group at the cost of a more productive agricultural system. Does this make developmental sense? No! Political sense? Yes!! What are the tradeoffs? You in this room will continually be asked to decide as you hopefully participate in the decision-making process. I have no simple answers for you. You will have to find them yourselves, and I sincerely hope that you will.

When he read this to Fr. Joseph Brown, SJ; Ph. D. Professor, Author, Priest, and lifelong friend of Reg in June 2020, Fr. Brown was ecstatic and conferred that "…this is still relevant today. I must have a copy to share with the young people in the struggle right now…" Father Brown is an enigma in his own right. Born in East St. Louis, he would receive his B.A. in Philosophy from St. Louis University (1968), M.A. in

Creative Writing from Johns Hopkins University (1969), M.A. in Afro-American Studies from Yale University (1983), and Ph. D. in American Studies from Yale University (1984). He was ordained as a Jesuit Priest in 1972. Father Brown is currently a Professor in the Department of Africana Studies at Southern Illinois University at Carbondale. Another branch of the Petty tree! And when the two of them get together to talk on any topic, be prepared to be enthralled and a literal captive audience for hours to come…

## Renaissance Man…

A man of many gifts and talents, Reg took on the mantle of publisher and editor for a newspaper of the world's youth called *Your World: an international paper for young people*. The mantra for this circulation was his truth:

> **Your World** is a newspaper that has an international focus for young people. It features articles on world issues, famous people, youth, global activities, geography, history, social studies, art, theater, sports, and other news of interest. It also offers reviews of books and records, information on clubs for youth, travel information and opportunities to make individual contact through letters to the editors.

*Your World* was published by Reg while he served as President of Educational Resources International (ERI), Incorporated. (All rights reserved. Reproductions without permission is prohibited.) The assistant editors were Ann Richardson, Sandy Clifford, Robert Devlin, and wife Lucy Petty. The consultants were Eugene Martin and Kevin Clements, Student Advisory Group.

Each volume came with a companion teacher/parent guide to give adults the tools to enhance the message of the articles. The cover page for one volume is below:

*Jaye P. Willis*

TEACHER AND PARENT GUIDE

Activities and discussion questions for each article in this issue of YOUR WORLD are suggested in this Teacher's Guide. Please do not feel limited by our suggestions or that you have to construct a formal lesson around each article. You may simply decide to distribute the newspaper to students and to give them time to read it. Whichever way you use the paper, remember that we want your students to do the following:

o to enjoy reading YOUR WORLD.
o to feel it's their newspaper to which they can contribute.
o to be motivated to explore and to develop new areas of interest as well as academic skills.

**FOR PARENTS**

You can help your child enjoy and benefit from reading YOUR WORLD in the following ways:

1. Go through the paper with your child just to show him or her the stories that are contained in each issue.
2. Help your child to decide the stories that he or she would like to read. Then find the summary of each of the stories in this guide.
3. Help your child to learn the vocabulary words for the stories that he or she reads. You will find the words listed under vocabulary in the description of each story in this guide. You can then explain the meaning of these words to your child. You can also look up the words in a dictionary with your child so that he or she learns how to use the dictionary.

4. Encourage your child to read other newspapers, magazines, and books that might have topics similar to those found in YOUR WORLD.

**FOR TEACHERS**

**The Ballad of Manute Bol** (page 2)

Summary: This article is about Manute Bol who, at 7 feet 7 inches, is the tallest player in the National Basketball Association. Bol is a member of the Dinka nation, a tall people who live in southern Sudan. Until Bol began playing basketball six years ago, he lived the life of a nomadic herdsman.

Vocabulary: herdsman, popularity, status, frail, drafted, wingspan, rookie, phenomenally, adapting, nomadic

Related Activity: Have students look up Sudan in the encyclopedia. Once they have read about this country and its peoples, conduct a discussion of what they think the differences would be between Bol's life in Africa and his life now.

Just for Fun: Students may enjoy writing their own songs about a favorite athlete and performing them for the class.

Reg produced a detailed business plan for the expansion of the youth newspaper for nationwide distribution. Since commenced in January 1987, the newspaper was used in 50 school systems in the United States. It was published twice monthly from September through May (16 issues) and sold for $5.00 per year subscription. Per the business plan, the market analysis that preceded the initial publication identified 25 million students in the United States in grades 6-12 with no international supplementary in the form of a newspaper with a global focus. In addition to his service in the Peace Corps and the Advisory Council on VocEd, he further lists working with the governments of Egypt, Saudi Arabia, Botswana, Mali, Ghana, and Puerto Rico assisting them in the improvement of their education and manpower training. His consultant resume includes working with development organizations such as Africare, the African Development Foundation and the US Agency on International Development. Though the newspaper was in print for several years and was an international beacon to many American students, it ceased operation after a major health scare with its driving force.

## A Knight's Fall

Reg awoke and the sun shone brightly, just like the day before. As he went about his daily routine of educating the world on the beauty, majesty and dignity of Black folks, a childhood malady was reemerging with a vengeance. Unclear of the moments before its arrival, a silent dark cloud enveloped Reg and placed him in suspended animation. It was about 1989. Reg and Lucy were living in Washington, DC. He had been working with brother Bruce Petty on several businesses, including Pettbros, Inc., a respected consulting firm in Washington, DC.

At approximately 54 years of age, Reg fell into a coma after suffering a severe seizure. He would remain in and out of this state for three months, suffering additional seizures. The prognosis was not good. As Reg recalls when he awoke, he found himself in a local hospital in Washington, DC. The doctors were not optimistic and as he recalled, told him that he had only a few months to live. They diagnosed him with an early onset of dementia with unknown etiology. To add to this drama, he and Lucy were facing foreclosure on their home, after missing three mortgage payments in October – December 1988. Also, one of the children required a great deal of hospitalization and had to undergo expensive treatments. These illnesses wiped out their savings and with Reg being unable to work, caused a tremendous strain on their income.

Karma entered through a letter from two of Reg's former Peace Corps volunteers – Joseph Permetti (Kenya) and Kevin Clements (Swaziland) to their peers, requesting financial support for the man who had, in many cases, helped to positively shape and change their lives forever. This is the true measure of a man's impact, when others generously come to his aid in times of trouble. The letter was dated 27 July 1989. One of the most compelling lines was as follows: "...This appeal is made by a group of volunteers who served under Reg and remember him to be a dynamic leader, and more importantly, the friend he was to each of us during our Peace Corps experience." Their efforts were successful in aiding the Petty's to retain their home.

The shock of the prognosis made Reg truly pensive and determined. He knew what he had to do. He headed home, to East Saint Louis, Illinois. By now, his father had died, and his mother was living in Rosewood Nursing Home in Fairview Heights, Illinois. He wanted to come home to share the vast experiences and world knowledge that he had amassed throughout his half century of living. A life lived nationally and abroad with experiences and contacts that only a small minority of his hometown peers had known. Before dying, Reg wanted to live again in East Saint Louis. His second marriage had deteriorated by this time and was coming to its conclusion.

He began working with local entities, like the Lessie Bates Neighborhood House. This is a local United Methodist Community Center that services families with activities from early childhood development to family support and economic development. Their goals were so aligned with what he had been doing for years that it seemed a perfect fit to work with them to reach the community. There he wrote proposals and organized workshops, helping to support their common cause.

Reg is one who sees a need and makes a plan to fill it. He saw the decay of the city's massive multi-story library, built in the late 1800's and housing an amazing collection of history. I imagine he saw this and thought of the great library of Alexandria. He became a one-man crew on a mission to save the artifacts within the library. By this time, many windows had been broken so the elements were invading this sacred space. Additionally, the building had become an illegal refuge for drug addicts, hookers and homeless of the city. Reg and a few of his friends braved the danger and removed hundreds of books from the library, including some rare and valuable books like phone records and yearbooks. A local storage company was used to house the books with the cooperation of the mayor and city leaders. Unfortunately, over time, these efforts were made waste as the storage payments were not kept up by the city and the owner is now difficult to locate. As we continue to search for the disposition of the owner and the materials within, we fear they have not fared well. These are the types of heroic efforts that must not just be made but manifest into a long-term and sustainable measure for the preservation of history.

One of the more impressive activities that Reg took part of in the early 90's had tremendous global impact. On June 5, 1991, Reg received correspondence from Secretary General Alfred Nzo of the African National Congress (ANC) inviting him to the ANC National Conference in Durban, South Africa, from July 3-6, 1991. Also invited per Reg's request was East St. Louis National Association for the Advancement of Colored People (NAACP) president Johnny Scott, Illinois House of Representatives member Wyvetter Younge, and then East St. Louis Mayor Gordon Bush. Reg was the only one able to make the trip. His observations were thought provoking:

> "...Apartheid had just ended, and the country was a mess. The ANC was in charge of the politics, but the white South Africans were still in charge of the money, land, diamonds, and gold mines. It was messy. There was even talk of a black civil war."

Reg met with Nelson Mandela and Bishop Desmond Tutu, along with other leaders to discuss the best methods to effect the transition of power. One of the most glaring missing pieces was black accountants. That skillset did not exist in the numbers needed to effectively run the country and had to be brought in for support. Reg was able to leverage his expertise to help stand up the new government. How amazing to be asked to assist and then be able to be a productive part of the solution! Looking at the country now, it is safe to say that Reg's input was positive, timely and effective.

On a side note, one paragraph of the correspondence discussed the travel arrangements to Durban in July. My ignorance of the geography immediately made me think that it would be super-hot in South Africa in July. However, the correspondence read:

> "The port-city of Durban is relatively warm during the period May-July whilst temperatures vary between minus zero degrees Celsius to twenty degrees in other parts of the country. Johannesburg in particular can be extremely cold during this time. It would be advisable to bring warm clothing along."

This made me think how wonderful it would have been for me to have the *Your World* newspaper as a youth, allowing me to think beyond my preconceptions!

## Introducing Edna...

Edna Patterson lived in East St. Louis. She was a graduate of Southern Illinois University at Edwardsville with a Bachelor of Fine Arts in Art and Design and a Master of Fine Arts in Art Therapy. She was divorced from her first husband with whom she had five children. She recalled their relationship as "very abusive", but her survival of the abuse made her stronger and spurred her desire to go to college to achieve her dreams of becoming an artist. She wanted to be an artist her whole life, even when she did not receive the support of her dreams from her family. She remembers quilting with her grandmother and finding solace in those times.

The first time that Edna met Reg was at the Lessie Bates Neighborhood House in East St. Louis. She recalls having heard of Reg, but she did not know him. She remembers once that he was supposed to receive an award, but he did not show up. Typical Reg. That was the first time that she heard his name. At Lessie Bates, Edna was looking for someone to work with the children on an African Art project for public school district 189. Reg kept asking Edna to come over to her home, but she did not know him and found him to be a little aggressive. He wanted to bring her some of his African art, so he laid it on the floor and said "…acquaint yourself with this and I'll see you tomorrow." He came back at 8:00 am the next day and they did their first workshop together.

Her first impression of him was that he was 'weird' and overly trusting of her. She was very candid with Reg about her abusive first marriage and her not wanting to rush into any relationship. They worked together for a year before they would start dating, with neither trying to impress the other during this period. Edna had been divorced for three years and Reg had been separated from Lucy that same amount of time. Photo of Reg and Edna was taken by Roland Freeman.

When Edna's eldest daughter, Angie, met Reg, they were at dinner. She asked him "What are your intentions with my Mom?" She found his daughter Amina's number and called her to get a better sense of this man. Her youngest son asked him "Did he play mind games?" Patches liked him so the other son was fine. The other children and grandchildren loved him also. Edna reminisces that Reg bought her granddaughter Brittany a pound of green grapes and she was hooked on him ever since.

Alberta Willis, Petty, Edna, Helen Petty.
Photo by Roland Freeman.

Edna quips that Reg asked her to marry him so many times that she finally said 'yes'! They were married on January 31, 1992 and have passed the quarter century mark! Amina remarked that Reg and Edna's marriage lasted even longer than her parents.

Friends David Levine and wife Judith Katz attended the wedding. Judith wrote a very moving note to the couple upon returning to Washington, DC and reflecting on the event and the experiences leading up to it. Excerpts are below:

> February 15, 1992
>
> Dear Reg and Edna,
>
> Since returning home from the wedding I have been flooded with emotions, images, and thoughts I wanted to share with you. First of all, your wedding was inspirational – a very special event in my life, my marriage with David, and my relationship with each of you. The love I feel from you, the strength of who you are in your own rights, and the power of your joining are very strong…
>
> …I keep reflecting on the seeming contradictions of coming to the wedding. The strength of your community wanting to celebrate your journey and

this important rite of passage in your lives. The power of creating an African American ceremony – the beauty surrounding the dancers, the drums, the beautiful dresses you made, Edna, the coming together of the community, the people's faces of celebration and love.

This was in sharp contrast to our experience prior to arriving at the church. Leaving the hotel, the racism and negative attitudes about East St. Louis were overt. Comments from both whites and blacks questioned why we were going there and warned us that it was not safe. No one knew directions – to them, East St. Louis was an undifferentiated area, not people who live in hard circumstances, part of forgotten America, struggling without an economic base, and with little hope for change. On reflection, the comments sounded much like those describing the third world – unsafe, unclean, an undifferentiated mass, unknown…

…Metaphorically, to equate a US city with the third world is one thing; to see it, feel it, experience it not as a metaphor but as a reality was quite another… This is a part of America few of us see; we want to keep our eyes shut. Perhaps this is what the people at the hotel were saying – "Why would you want to go there?" How much easier it is to pretend this part of America is not real…

…And yet, another side of the power of the trip was seeing East St. Louis through your eyes. Reg, as you describe the different parts of the town, I was taken by your ability to see the potential, to see the possibilities for development, to understand the complexities of life – trying to make change – the trade-offs of drugs, poverty and violence, and the power of collective action. I admire your ability not to feel hopeless or victimized but carve out a place for yourselves to serve as a catalyst in the community. The spirit and power of the Black church, always at the center of change for the African American community, is very much alive in you…

…There are several lessons that I take from my time with you. Your relationship serves to strengthen what you bring to others – each of you in your way serving as a guide to help us find our inner voice, to find our spirit, and to use our faith and energy so that we are victims no more. Searching to overcome oppression is not about sophisticated programs -- it is about acts of courage and commitment joined together. For me, our friendship and being with you on this special occasion has served to strengthen my own resolve. We must, each in our own way, find our voices, and join in the journey.

This letter helps to underscore the title of the book. The pandemic is not about a virus but the mindset of people who marginalize entire groups of people as disposable, unforgettable, and not worth the energy to understand. But Judith describes the hope that is possible when eyes and minds are opened to humanity.

Reg and Edna have a lot in common, including their love of East St. Louis, Illinois, a love of history, truth about the people and the arts. They desire to expose youth to history and travel. One time they took a group of children to Washington, DC. They went to the Art museums and the Wax museum.

Edna describes the most important gift that Reg ever gave her, increased self-confidence. Her self-esteem was non-existent. Reg believed in her until she could believe in herself again. Edna recalled once that they were traveling from Washington, DC and Reg asked her to drive. She was fearful of being judged (like her ex-husband would do). Reg was kind and supportive and even went to sleep during part of the drive, empowering her to successfully make the trip home.

Reg's tough love for Edna was truly put to the test when Edna was offered an opportunity to travel to Africa. She wanted Reg to come with her as he had been and lived there years before. She knew that he could show her the sights and most of all help ease her fears of being so far from him. But Reg had other ideas. He wanted her to experience Africa on her own, through her eyes and emotions and not his. He wanted her to absorb the essence of her surroundings through her artistic senses, which he was sure would alleviate any fears she might face in this new land. In listening to Edna recount her experiences in Africa, one understands why Reg did what he did. Edna went from being angry and afraid to grateful.

    I have found this to be the real gift of Reg. Being a first-time author, I had many occasions to fear my ability to do justice to his life story. But Reg continued to challenge me to face my fears and finish the book, telling me "Whenever you finish is when it was supposed to be done. Keep going."

## Boards and Accolades

In true Reg Petty style, he became engrossed in serving his community. And as more people realized that he was home for good, they began reaching out to him for his service. In 1992, Reg served as the Executive Director of the Metro East Church-Based Citizens' Organization (M.E.C.C.O.). The board sought to encompass all religious entities in the city, including Baptists, Catholics, Lutherans, Methodists, Church of God in Christ and Non-denominational. Reg was a much sought-after executive for many other boards due to his wide experiences in consulting throughout the world. In 2002, esteemed anthropologist and benefactress of East St. Louis, Madame Katherine Dunham, reached out to Reg for his service with the following words:

> "...In the interest of maintaining a high level of effectiveness and fiscal responsibility in programs I have developed throughout the years, I am reconstituting the Board for the Katherine Dunham Centers for Arts and Humanities. As one who has shown a high level of interest in maintaining

my legacy in East St. Louis and elsewhere, and in promoting goals of community education and intercultural communication, I am inviting you to share in pursuing those aims as a board member of the Centers..."

Her enigmatic original signature is on the letter dated August 1, 2002. That makes the request even more special. She did not have her secretary prepare the request and rubber stamp her signature. This extra effort conveyed her true desire to have this learned man on the Board of Directors of her Centers.

Reg participated in numerous speaking engagements throughout the year, but February was truly his busiest month, for obvious reasons. Whenever Reg made a presentation, he would also bring African artifacts with him as an aide in the learning process. For instance, in February 1993, Reg was the keynote speaker for the YMCA of Greater St. Louis, invited by Lynda Burgman, Senior Vice-President, Financial Development. His topic was 'Experiences in the African Peace Corps" and consisted of several pieces of his collected African artwork. Reg received similar accolades from Richard "R.J." Krause for this presentation to the St. Clair County's Teachers Institutes in St. Clair County, Illinois.

That same month, he received accolades from notable educator Johnetta Haley, Director of the Southern Illinois University Edwardsville (SIUE) East St. Louis Center and Vice President of the East St. Louis Community Fund, for his work over the past year with the funds Interest-Free Education Loan Program. As a result of Reg's volunteer efforts, 46 students received interest-free education loans. The positive impact of Reg returning home and sharing his knowledge, skills and abilities was growing by leaps and bounds and the citizens were thrilled.

One person who captured this thrill was Mr. Victor Little. Mr. Little performed the play *Crowns of Glory* at the University of Missouri – St. Louis, in April 2002, during the Multi-Cultural Week Celebration at the campus. After the performance, Reg presented him with an African straw hat from the country of Benin. In Mr. Little's words from an appreciation letter to Reg, "…It is more precious to me than you could ever have known, and I thank you for your kindness…" These little acts of kindness from Reg spark intensity in the recipients, making them want to do more, learn more, and overall improve upon themselves and those around them. I know I feel that way every time we meet or talk.

In a similar fashion, Patsy Mix Gillis, was moved by her purchase of Reg's book *Bits & Pieces of East St. Louis*, stating how professionally researched it was. She also expanded her family's heritage in East St. Louis from their business cited in the book. This sharing of information both within the family and with others expands the history of the city, which is a primary goal of Reg.

Petty at a meeting in Washington, DC. Photo from the Petty archives.

Petty with Lucy, sons Anthony and Joel, and daughter Amina. Photo by Roland Freeman from Petty archives.

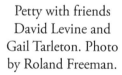

Petty with friends David Levine and Gail Tarleton. Photo by Roland Freeman.

Petty hugging mom Helen with Lucy looking on. Photo by Roland Freeman.

Wedding photo with Edna and Mother-in-law Helen Petty. Photo by Roland Freeman.

Wedding photo with Joel Petty, Grandmother Helen, and Edna's Mom Alberta Willis. Photo by Roland Freeman.

*Jaye P. Willis*

## **Night Crying**
*By Reginald Petty*

Night crying, soundlessly, possessively,
When all is finite, purifying self-delusions,
Wet sheets from ejaculation of tears,
Primitive, mocking, futuristic ideas
Thimble of water quenching the thirst for
Happiness for those not yet born

# FOUR SCORE

# Pandemic Parle

(61-80) 1996-2015

### Cradle to the Brave
*Praise Song Sonnet for Reginald Petty*

*Born in bigotry, severed, unequal,*
*Hospital acceptance focused on hue.*
*Their practice akin to bovine fecal,*
*Suppressing service by ocular view.*

*With belief that he and Mom passed for white,*
*Light skin and hazel eyes confused this child,*
*Thinner than peers, standing shorter in height,*
*Intellect heavy with demeanor wild.*

*Grown up bachelor conquered his masters,*
*Registered Southern voters through jail doors.*
*Taught self-reliance through pundit plaster*
*Chess drummers work led to Job and Peace Corps.*

*Evil is quenched through humanity drought*
*While genius of a good man triumphs bout.*

—*By Jaye P. Willis*

It was during this time that Reg gathered all his experiences through national and international travels, work, and knowledge gained to transfer that information to pliant minds he charged to carry on the work of his generation.

In 2002, Reg served as an agency representative for the East St. Louis Renaissance Literary Arts Press. He, along with grant writer Vann E. Ford, successfully pursued a grant from the Enterprise Community Vision 20/20 group for a National Endowment for the Arts (Federal) grant for the city of East St. Louis, Illinois. The primary goal of the grant was to sponsor a week-long Miles Davis Arts Festival in the city, to include art shows, poetry readings/contests, artist workshops, literary panel discussions, creation of outdoor art murals, and an eight-hour music concert. The program was an unmitigated success and written about prominently in the local newspapers, including the St. Louis Post Dispatch and the Belleville News Democrat.

On August 3, 2002, the African Family Film Foundation founder and Executive Director, Taale Laafi Rosellini, reached out to Reg to help them review their budget and assist them to secure funding for a 105-minute video edit of **Great Great Great Grandparents' Music** – the documentary about the remarkable Kone family of musicians in West Africa, filmed over a period of two decades. Reg's expertise is well documented and sought after by many on local and global matters. The letter ends with the phrase 'Wend na kont f nyo woko!' which translates to 'May the Great Spirit give you long life!'

Recuperation from his health scare was still in the forefront of his and Edna's minds. Reg used this time to delve into his most prolific skill – research. He began an intensive historical research of his beloved hometown of East St. Louis, Illinois. This included going to libraries and going through books, newspaper archives, microfilm and microfiche, and whatever documentation existed on the subject. He interviewed other historians like Professor Andrew Theising with Southern Illinois University at Edwardsville and served as a historian for Sandra Pfeifer who would complete her documentary *Against All the Odds: A Documentary of East St. Louis, Illinois* in 2017. He also spoke with Pastors, Priests,

Centenarians, Business Owners, and the folks in the streets – anyone who could give him the information that he needed. From these discussions, Reg wrote his next book "Bits & Pieces of East St. Louis History", in 2004. The book identifies East St. Louis history from 1890 – 2004, in bits and pieces from resources he was able to gather. Edna and Fay Suber served as editors. It consisted of directories of schools and churches, businesses, teachers and business leaders, city officials and federal census data from 1880, 1890 and 1900. There is even a listing of Colored Population in 1903, names A-K, and Heroes and Sheroes from 1970 – 2004.

Staff writer Linda Lawson of the local newspaper, the East St. Louis Monitor, wrote an article on Mr. Petty entitled *City's historical sleuth tracks down its roots*. She quoted Mr. Petty as saying, "I am a firm believer that if you don't know where you've been, you can't tell where you are going." The article chronicles his path to the history of the city, including the aforementioned abandoned library and the rescue of the books, some dating as far back as the 1800's.

A large part of his research on the 1917 race riot in East St. Louis consisted of reaching profound works like

- *The Crisis*, Vacation Number August 1917, from the Indiana University Library, Vol. 14 – No.4, Whole No. 82. Multiple sections addressed the race riot, including the section The Looking Glass, pages 175-179.
- The Crisis, September 1917, provided a double East St. Louis Number - Edition 43,000. It was full of documentation related to the Central Trades and Labor Union letter calling for action to be taken against the mass migration of the Negro from Mississippi to East St. Louis, photos of affected Negroes from the riots like Narcis Gurley and Mineola McGee, the fire that raged, and the Negro silent walk at 42nd Street and Fifth Avenue in New York City.
- The Modernist Journals Project, a joint project of Brown University and The University of Tulsa.
- An article from Ida B. Wells-Barnett written in the Chicago Defender July 1917. Mrs. Wells-Barnett traveled to East St. Louis on July 3, 1917, to see the aftermath of the riots first-hand.

- The Negro Fellowship League of Chicago, Illinois, passed a resolution on the state of affairs during the East St. Louis riot in July 1917.
- Riot At East St. Louis, Illinois. Hearings before Committee on Rules, House of Representatives, Sixty-Fifth Congress, First Session on H. J. Res. 118, August 3, 1917
- *East St. Louis Toodle-Oo* song by Duke Ellington and Bub Miley

Reg took all this research and additional documentation and interviews to create a comprehensive roadmap to the riot activities. Therefore, he wears the hat or should I say kufi, of East St. Louis Historian.

## A Living Trust

A recurring theme in Reg's life is his being a trustworthy man. In each interview I conducted over the past four years, that question has been at the forefront: *When did you develop trust with Reg?* In one instance, though, I was not able to ask this question. It was a situation of action speaking louder than words.

Many famous musicians were born, raised, and played in East St. Louis, IL. One of them was a man named Eugene Haynes. Like Reg, Eugene Haynes was born into segregation, with his birthplace being St. Louis, MO in 1927, but his rearing in East St. Louis, IL. Eugene became an internationally renowned classical pianist, studying at the Julliard School in New York with friend Miles Davis. **Challenge – Learn more about the lives of these two great musicians from East St. Louis.**

After attending Julliard, Eugene would briefly attend the historically black college and university (HBCU), Lincoln University in Jefferson City, MO, located in the state capital, where, later, he was Artist in Residence. Eugene then lived, learned, and played in Paris, France and Denmark. He spent much of his time in Europe as his home country was not as accepting of his talent as a black man. Unfortunately, this was a common theme amongst many African American artists during the early to middle 1900's.

He would also come home and spend time with his close friends, one of whom was Reginald Petty. When Eugene died in 2007, he left his diaries and papers to Reg. Now if that ain't trust, I do not know what is!

In accordance with his wishes, Reg donated the Eugene Haynes Collection to Lincoln University in Jefferson, City, MO, where it remains today for future classical pianists and lovers of history and music to study. In 2008, Reg received a letter from then president of Lincoln University, Dr. Carolyn Mahoney, thanking him for entrusting the collection to the university. A prolific life teacher in his own right, Reg understood that this collection belonged to the world to enlighten and encourage others and did not hold it for his own private collection or gain. In 2016, I had an opportunity to visit Lincoln University during homecoming (my daughter Lauren is a 2013 graduate) and was allowed to view the Eugene Haynes collection. It is meticulously housed in the library and quite inspiring to see.

Reg was approached by members of Eugene's adopted country of Denmark to receive artifacts from his collection. Reg believed that Lincoln University would be the best place for these items where the youth of his hometown and other African American youth could learn and be inspired by his story and greatness.

Reg believes that his legacy will be perceived as follows:

1. The people he has positively touched and impacted
2. Living his life with certain values and concerns
3. Attempts to change/improve conditions for others
4. Not measuring his legacy by what he has changed but what he has done
5. His support of Edna's artwork
6. His love for his children, family, and community

*Jaye P. Willis*

# A Dynamic Duo

Reg and Edna wanted to make a positive impact on East St. Louis through Art and History. One of their joint ventures was P &P Enterprises, where they developed a concept paper for an international teacher's resource guide. The paper described the initiative as "...an opportunity for communities to leverage their resources of individuals, small businesses, corporations, and other groups who could provide information to students, teachers, and administrators regarding the economic and socio-psychological impact of the globalization of their community and the world." Much like the *Your World* newspaper, they hoped to share information on what was happening in other parts of the world to open the eyes of young people and their instructors to see their situation through another lens.

As word was getting around about P & P Enterprises, both Edna and Reg were sought after to make presentations to youth and adult audiences alike. One such request came from the YMCA of Greater St. Louis in St. Louis, Missouri, asking Reg to speak at their 1993 International Conference being held at Washington University's Simon Hall.

I believe that Reg's life is encapsulated in fighting against the dystopian societies often linked to George Orwell books like *Animal Farm* and *Nineteen Eighty-four (1984)*. America post-slavery and the "freed" Blacks underscore this dystopian society which extends into Ronald Reagan's America. Jesse Jackson led a coastal grass roots face-to-face discussion with America on behalf of U.S. Presidential Candidate Walter Mondale in 1984 – *coincidence*... Reg was among a select group speaking on the crisis in South Africa, a topic that he was intimately familiar with as a Peace Corps Director in Swaziland.

On December 16, 2004, the Belleville News Democrat published an article on History from a Black Perspective, based on the books "Bits & Pieces of East St. Louis History" and "East St. Louis Area Revisited". The article reported that ...*Petty doesn't see his books as East St. Louis histories but as reference materials that could be used by other researchers who have the time, energy, and inclination to take on a major project*... By this time, Reg was 69 and recovering from quadruple heart bypass surgery. He wanted to present the data and information as a challenge to someone or group of people to follow through on some or all aspects of his research. To note, even in 2020, there is still more work to do with this reference material. Any takers? Another treasure from the article was a large picture of four young African American women dressed very professionally and standing shoulder to shoulder. They were from Reg's vast collection of photos and were identified as Dr. Carrie Dawson, Beatrice Hunter Neeley, Helen Petty (Reg's mother) and an unidentified woman.

During this 20-year period, Reg spent a tremendous amount of time on speaking engagements throughout the Metropolitan St. Louis area and abroad. He attended a conference in Canada with wife Edna, where he was asked to present in French. Though he had not spoken French in years, he was able to make his way through the presentation to everyone's delight. As Reg was approaching Social Security age during this time, he appropriately paced himself with his activities, but the seizures and blackouts continued, though not frequently but enough to let him know that he had to take it easier these days. He would continue to meet with local and state officials to share history, advocate for groups, and keep East St. Louis history on the minds of those in charge, like Mayors Gordon Bush and Alvin Parks, Jr., along with County Assessor Percy McKinney, Illinois State Senators James Clayborne, Jr. and Christopher Belt, U.S. Senator Richard "Dick" Durbin and Illinois State Representatives Jerry Costello, LaToya Greenwood and Jay Hoffman. He frequently meets with St. Clair County Board Chairman and friend, Mark Kern, to discuss matters of East St. Louis and its position in the county.

In 1984, Mondale was the first candidate to select a woman running mate in Geraldine Ferraro, citing that she was "…far better prepared for her position than Mr. Reagan was when he was elected president of the United States." Mondale's progressive attitude towards a woman candidate showed a positive change in female equality in this country. Reg concurred that women should take their seat at the governing table, as they would most assuredly be overqualified just to be considered.

*Jaye P. Willis*

## **East St. Louis Winners & Losers**

*By Reginald Petty*

Growing up Black-You
Need a little Slack
Smack
And plenty Jack
Wasn't all fun, never knew who won
I was always stunned
From other folks gun
Laughed and cried, laughed, and cried
Laughed and cried
Tried to hide, always tried to hide
In plain sight
Full of fright
Always tight
Ready for a fight
Never knew who Won

# FIVE SCORE

# Eternal Vigil

### (81+) 2016 -

### Reflective Agitator
(a kwansaba tribute poem)

*Time takes the baton as waking hours
decline for our native son, rising 'round
noon from restive slumber laurel-filled
pallet. With psyche poised to pound veiled
in-equity descent of Jefferson, eternal vigil
exposed through pensive eyes and sensual tone,
our hero wields wisdom, slaying Grand Dragons*
—By Jaye P. Willis

### Perpetual Motion

While many octogenarians are at home partaking of that long overdue rest on a mound of their laurels, Mr. Petty continues to work on adding value to human rights causes. He is a very sought-after speaker for Black History Month programs throughout the metropolitan St. Louis Area. In

2017, dear friend Alice Windom and Reg attended a program in East St. Louis sponsored by their mutual friend, Dr. Eugene Benjamin Redmond, through his writer's club. The performing arm of the club is known as the Soular Systems Ensemble (of which I am a proud member). "Soular" is a neologism. Before and after the performance, I had the opportunity to meet with Alice and Reg to discuss their times together. They reminisced about the McCarthy Hearing of October 1962 where Lola Bell Holmes reported. And on friends Charles and Margaret Burroughs who started the DuSable Museum in their basement before it moved to the Field Museum. They also spoke fondly on Mr. F.H. Hamurabi who provided African lectures in Chicago.

Petty with legendary friend Alice Windom and me.
Photo by Ros Crenshaw.

The Pettys live in a modest home in East St. Louis but to many of us, it is as regal as any castle in Eastern Europe. It is a two-story home with a basement, but not just your average craftsman style home. Every room is a work of art and is one of the grandest entertaining spots in the city. The Petty's have hosted book signings, birthday parties, college students, dignitaries, and millionaires in their home. I had the privilege of attending the book signing of author Michael Datcher, whose book, *Americus*, dramatically elicits early 20th century plights in East St. Louis, Illinois.

The year 2017 was a critical time in East St. Louis as it marked the 100th anniversary of the infamous East St. Louis, Illinois 1917 race riots about which his elders had spoken to him as a child. For historical purposes, let me set the scene in 1917. East St. Louis was a booming industrial town, with railroads, stockyards, and glass and ore industry. Many of the town's residents were white European emigrants (Polish, German, etc.) who had come here because of available jobs. These were good paying jobs, and the city began to flourish. At the same time, the great migration of Blacks from the South to the North was taking place. They, too, had heard of the jobs in East St. Louis and wanted to share in this prosperity. At first, this addition of citizens was accepted as the numbers were small. The strike of white workers at the Aluminum Ore plant in the city became the catalyst for events to come. The Ore company management brought in Black workers to replace the striking White workers. This led to meetings of the labor union to address how to stop management from the hirings. Civil unrest ensued, bringing such notable civil rights activists as Ida B. Wells-Barnett and W.E.B. DuBois to the city.

In 2016, then Mayor Alvin Parks, Jr. commissioned a group to develop activities within the city to remind the citizens and everyone else of the atrocities that took place during that time, but also where we are now and where we need to go in the future. It was named the East St. Louis 1917 Centennial Commission Cultural Initiative, Inc. (EStL 1917 CCCI). In 2017, the Commission held several culturally impactful events to educate people on what happened in 1917, a history lesson unfortunately not taught in the city's educational curriculum.

It is no surprise that both Reg and Edna were asked to be commissioners on this initiative. Reg brought his rich history of the city to the table and Edna created unique and poignant art worthy to be housed in the finest museums. They worked tirelessly with dear friend Fr. Joseph Brown, who was named head of the Commission. The Commission's long work and efforts bore much fruit, including new signage in the city identifying "Sacred Sites", which were 24 points of interest where specific events took place. In January 2017, at St. Louis

Community College in St. Louis, Missouri, a rally of poetry, dance and speeches were delivered.

Other commemorative rallies took place at the East St. Louis Higher Education building in May and July of 2017. This was one of the sites where the events of 1917 took place. They included townhall meetings and a march across the Eads Bridge, where many Blacks tried to escape the horrific violence from East St. Louis, Illinois to St. Louis, Missouri. The commission was quick to clarify that the events of 1917 should not be called "race riots" but a pogrom, which is defined as "an organized massacre." As the blacks in the city were unarmed and did not precipitate the violence but were its victims, this could not be called a riot. Another fruit of the commission was the creation of the *I Am East St. Louis* magazine, a free community-based publication that covers positive news about the city. Initially published bi-monthly (now quarterly), the magazine highlights the rich accomplishments of East St. Louisans, both past and present. It was the brainchild of Retired U. S. Naval Commander Charmaine Savage, who served as its founder and editor, and her adoring husband, Lorenzo Savage, an architect also from East St. Louis. To learn more about the commission, visit https://www.estl1917ccci.us To order the magazine, visit www.iamestl.com

The pairing of Reg and Charmaine was cosmic. Reg had a vast array of contacts with influential city natives, like U.S. Ambassador Donald McHenry and Sports Educator Dr. Harry Edwards. Reg contacted his friends and Charmaine jetted off to meet and interview them. On the first Saturday evening of December 2016, Charmaine held the inaugural I Am East St. Louis banquet at the Casino Queen hotel. It was a magical night that took lots of preparation and planning. I was humbled to be called by Charmaine earlier that summer to ask me to work with her on identifying the first award honoree for the magazine. Of course, we both agreed that it should be none other than Reginald Petty! I was charged with interviewing his friends and colleagues to create a video of well-wishers. This included travelling to Washington, DC to meet with Peace Corps co-workers Tom Fox and David Levine. I locally met with childhood friends Willie Currie, Curtis Paradise, and Mary Cannon. I contacted his children, Tony, Joel, and Amina to invite them to the celebration. Charmaine worked with the Peabody Awards staff to create an award with the likeness of Mr. Petty to be presented to him and future award winners, naming it the Reginald Petty Service Award.

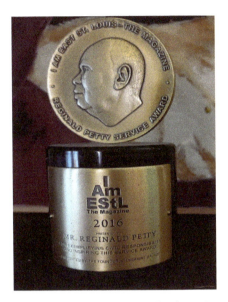

*I Am EStL* Reginald Petty Service Award. Photo by Jaye P. Willis

He was both surprised and humbled as his friends and family arrived, including David Levine and his wife, Judith Katz, and Reg's children Joel and Amina Petty and their significant others. I prepared the voice over for the video and accomplished videographer Michael Franks put it all together. The tears of joy and accomplishment were all over his face, as captured by numerous photographers, including my son, then photography student Jered R. Willis. Charmaine even featured one of Jered's photographs of the event in the magazine, giving him his first professional magazine credit.

*Jaye P. Willis*

# PUBLISHER'S NOTE

*IAmEStL* magazine publisher's Charmaine and Lorenzo Savage, with Petty at the magazines inaugural ball. Photo by Jered Willis.

Not to be overlooked for his artistic side, Reg challenged or commanded me (depends on how I choose to look at it) to create a play of the 1917 pogrom and to have it ready for presentation in October 2017, 100 years to the date of the trials held in the city related to the incidents. As I am unable to say 'no' to Reg, I worked with him and solicited a cast to perform in **The Phoenix Trials: A Semi historical Play of the 1917 Pogrom in East St. Louis, Illinois**. It was a tremendous help to me to have access to the years of research that Reg had previously completed. The daunting task was reading through everything and identifying what we would use for the play.

Our cast consisted of a retired judge, an actress, a poet, a professional dancer, and a myriad of other ordinary folks, coming together for an extraordinary event, all at the bequest of myself via my tether to Reginald Petty. There were two performances at the East St. Louis Senior High School in their Katherine Dunham Performing Arts Center, which houses the Miles Davis Theatre. It was not an easy fete to accomplish but whenever I wavered or doubted myself, Reg was there to encourage and lift me. We are both immensely proud of the play and the community that helped to make the event happen.

Petty and me (holding poster) with the cast (L-R) Quintin Willis, Jered Willis, Tasha Shannon, Gigi Campbell, Bob Gill, Emani Jennings, Lawanda Young, Retired Judge Milton Wharton, Daphne Dorsey, Kevin Harris, Jerome Harris, Charlois Lumpkin, Paulette Shipp, Roosevelt Wilson, Mary Cannon, and Valerie Adams. Not pictured is Jimmy Rice.

The next year, our dear sister Charmaine Savage succumbed to breast cancer at the age of 51, but her legacy and the magazine continue through the efforts of her husband and friends with continued and new subscriptions.

Professor Eugene B. Redmond, poet laureate of East St. Louis, routinely calls on his friend Reg to speak at our regularly scheduled Soular System Ensemble events. EBR, as he is affectionately called, previously lived in Africa, and taught prominent African American authors, actors, poets, and visionaries. He is the author of Drumvoices: The Mission of Afro-American Poetry, A Critical History. If Reg is the griot, EBR is the soul of the city, and Fr. Joseph Brown the heart. When in their presence, you are caught up in a whirlwind of folklore, history, Black pride, humility, challenge, and grace – and you thank your Creator for the privilege. That trifecta is solid money, all day, every day.

## When Protégés Visit

Sitting in the inviting Afro-centric living room of Reginald and Edna Petty always elicits a sense of warmth and pride. On a cool September's day in 2019, two former Peace Corps volunteers who worked with Reg some 40 years earlier while he was Country Director in Swaziland stopped by to reminisce with him and share their stories with me. Kevin Clements lives in Atlanta. He worked with the World Bank and Southwestern Bell. He remembers that when he originally applied for the Peace Corps, his application was lost, and he was not interviewed. He tried again three months later. Reg read his application and contacted him. Reg made a few calls and then asked Kevin if he could be in Philadelphia by Saturday. From one Thursday to the next, Kevin was in Washington, DC to Philadelphia on his way to Swaziland!

Anne Latimer was a journalist in Chicago, Illinois. When she applied for the Peace Corps, her preference was to go to Ghana. She was sent to Mauritania, but they could not find a job for her. She became familiar with the Dima party, whose president was the wife of the Country Director. It was about 1978-79. Anne helped to develop tutoring instructions. Reg heard of her and reached out. She spoke some French and Siswati (soft language clicks). She became a volunteer in Swaziland.

The two volunteers shared joyful memories of the big Thanksgiving dinners Reg and his family would throw for the over 100 volunteers. The turkeys came from the Embassy. They remember one year that famed singer Chubby Checker came to dinner and singer Shirley Payne performed.

During their free time, the two remembered going to the Banzini (casino), horseback riding, and roasting meat and drinking beer under the stars. Some of the White volunteers would go to South Africa on their free weekends but the Blacks could not go as apartheid was alive and well then. Reg and the other Country Directors also discouraged the volunteers from going into South Africa. They also recalled that in Zimbabwe, Mozambique, and South Africa they feared for their lives, but not in Swaziland. Being so close to South Africa, things like having all their mail opened were not uncommon.

The volunteers were scattered all over the country in support of the locals but would come together for training and holiday events.

Anne remembers arriving at the Johannesburg airport wearing traditional West African garb and how the South Africans stared at her asking what she was wearing! For her to enter the airport, she was considered an "honorary White".

She also remembers a time when she, two Black males and a White female commandeered a car and went to the Seychelles (off of the coast of Kenya) for a New Year's concert. They were invited by the band. When they arrived, the hotel management asked them to leave as it was a Whites only event. It was 1980.

Reg, Kevin, and Anne shared a laugh about the 'flying fox' or fruit bats in the Seychelles. Both Kevin and Anne went to new countries and challenges after completing their Peace Corps tours in Swaziland. Anne would go to Mauritania from 1983-87, then back to the US to Champaign, Illinois. Kevin went to Zimbabwe from 1983-87, then Lagos, Nigeria from 1990-95. They reminisced more about the tribal groups in Nigeria, other Black volunteers, and how Reg had indelibly left an endearing mark on their lives. Anne's daughter Halima was with them.

Petty, Kevin, Anne and Halima on a 2019 visit to the Petty home. Anne is holding a poster of a quilt by Edna. Photo by Jaye P. Willis.

Watching them interact in a relaxed and peaceful environment and listening to their laughter was magical. I felt transported to their memories. More importantly, I saw the pride in Reg's face as he looked at his protégés, and I imagine, subconsciously realizing his impact on the success of his dear friends.

Reg never loses focus of the impact of all world citizens on each other. We do not live on this Earth alone but as humans; we live as a collective of beings whose actions have impact on one another. Hence, this man is the true epitome of the Pandemic Prophet – the one who has seen the effects of poverty, wealth, famine, disease, racism, bigotry, religion, classism, and other factors on communities of people worldwide and channels his life force to improve the human conditions affecting them, one group at a time. He leads the charge in alerting us that if we don't change our mindsets to be more inclusive and just, mankind will fall into a devastating pandemic that can wipe out our civilization.

*The Pandemic Prophet*

## Ever the Mentor

When Jered graduated from Webster University in St. Louis, Missouri in May 2018, with a degree in Communications and Studio Photography, he took the summer off to serve as Reg's personal driver. He took him to run errands and to community speaking engagements. Reg is a master of oral history and sought after to regale youth groups to senior peers, from novice historians to learned academia. Two of Reg's favorite places to present are the Christian Activity Center, a local center adjacent to a housing project, and the city's Higher Education Center which also houses the Charter High School. In these places, he shows the students items that he has amassed over his storied years, including his passports and African artifacts. Often hearing Reg's stories and seeing these items elicited wanderlust within the students and all who were present, including Jered.

Petty and Jered Willis. Photo by Jaye P. Willis.

During these short excursions, the two would discuss all manner of topic, including sports, music, manhood, world travel, service, and life. Reg became a life counselor to him and a sounding board for his future. When Jered came home and told me and his father that he wanted to join the Peace Corps to serve others in need and share his talents, we knew that Reg had imprinted his love of humanity and self-sacrifice on our son. We could not have been prouder of Jered. Though the coronavirus pandemic of 2020 halted his application process for the Peace Corps, he is not deterred from the mission.

Over the past four years, Reg has spoken at numerous events. One particular heavy presentation period was during the 50th Anniversary of the March 7, 1965 march across the Edmund Pettus Bridge in Selma, Alabama. Reg was there and marched across the bridge with friends John Lewis, Stokely Carmichael and Martin Luther King, Jr. US Congressman John Lewis came to East St. Louis several times in recent years: in 2016 he spoke at New Life in Christ Church where Kendall Granger is Pastor and was the guest speaker at the 2018 East St. Louis NAACP dinner in St. Louis, Missouri, where Stanley Franklin was President. Reg routinely spoke at the Sunshine Cultural Arts Center, named for Sylvester 'Sunshine' Lee. He received the nickname 'Sunshine' from former mentor Madam Katherine Dunham. Sylvester regards Reg as his 'Big Brother' and mentor. Reg and I served on the board of directors for the Center.

Reg even found time to write another book with local educator Tiffany Grimmett Lee, entitled **"Legendary East St. Louisans: An African American Series"** published in 2016. Again, highlighting the accomplishments of so many heroes and sheroes of a small town that per capita has made a huge impact both at home and abroad.

Reg turned 85 on October 7, 2020. My gift to him and his family is this completed book and my humble gratitude that they entrusted me to put his life's work in my voice. On this day, when I continue to work with Reg on the East St. Louis Historical Society, I know that there are more opportunities to add to this book. This will be the challenge for the next biographer; a pas de deux per se. As we spoke, he mentioned his call with fellow East St. Louisans Dr. Harry Edwards, and US Ambassador Donald McHenry, and Dr. Gloria Bozeman Herndon. Just to check the call log on his cell phone is a walk through history. He brings out the best in us and never stops moving forward, challenging us to step up and make a positive difference for those in need. As we excise those socioeconomic Guinea worms of our modern minds, we are now more cognizant to filter those negative thoughts of racism, sexism, classism, ageism, rich versus poor, educated versus undereducated, white collar versus blue collar, height shaming, body shaming, religious differences, and all the foolishness that separates us from being one human race with one Creator. This book is a call to find your better self and not be defined by your environment or fears. This is your approval to empower yourself to be the positive change that your home, neighborhood, community, city, county, state, nation, country, and world needs. Reginald Edwin Petty is not a saint or myth, but a man who embraced his destiny and said, "this is not acceptable, and I can make this better." No man, weapon or leader is bigger than the power within us to see what needs to be done and do it. I leave you love, peace, and a mission. Interpret that as you will.

Helen Petty. Photo from Petty archives.

Helen Petty with African artifacts from Petty. Photo from Petty archives.

Petty with influential friend Professor Eugene B. Redmond (far left). Photo taken after an annual Malcolm X memorial program at East St. Louis Senior High School. The program is sponsored by members of the East St. Louis Alumnae chapter of Delta Sigma Theta Sorority, Inc.: Dr. Lillian Parks, Mary Cannon, Curtis Louise Paradise, and Darlene Roy.

*The Pandemic Prophet*

Petty at St. Louis Art Museum in 2018 giving a discussion on crossing the Pettus bridge in Selma, Alabama in 1965. Photo from Petty archives.

Petty with brother Bruce. Photo from Petty archives.

Petty, Edna and Bruce with members of the Eugene B. Redmond Writer's Club. Photo from Petty archives.

*Jaye P. Willis*

Petty with youth from Creighton University in 2019 after a visit to his home. Their notes to him are below. Photo from Petty archives.

Thank you so much for your hospitality and welcoming us into your home. I loved learning about your experiences in the peace Corps and seeing all of the amazing artifacts. Your knowledge and experiences during the Civil Rights Movement was awesome to learn about. I wish you the best and I hope to make a difference alongside future generations. Love,
Katie

Thanks for opening your mind to us. The world is lucky to have your story etched in our timeline.
— Femi

Thank you for everything
— Fred Millan V

Thanks!!
— Connor

Mr. Petty —

Thank you so much for welcoming us into your home! It was such a joy being able to hear your knowledge. I loved the beauty in your house. Thank you for everything!
Love,
Jaylieen

Thank you so much for allowing us to come into your amazing home. You are such an incredible person & it was an honor to meet you. Thank you for opening our eyes. Thank you for everythink!
♥,
Dayna

## Old Men Tales
*By Reginald Petty*

Old men have strange thoughts, such as:
Both fact and fantasy bring forth love,
Authentic thought patterns merge to produce honesty,
Visions and past future determine the present,
All religions are true and false accidentally,
Power smells sour and selflessness rose petal sweet -
Fact, fantasy, visions merged to produce YOU

# EPILOGUE

There are some who may still wonder why the title of the book is the Pandemic Prophet. The pandemic that I refer to is not SARS or Coronavirus or any other bacterial or viral disease. The pandemic referenced in the title is specifically highlighted in the secondary name of the book; it is more sociological than physical. When man recognizes that there is an omnipotent Creator yet refuses to acknowledge the beauteous differences in their fellow man, or more arrogantly believes that their gifts are superior to those of another who is not identical to him, a shift results in their subconscious that leads to apparitions like racism, classism, sexism, homophobia, and intolerance. This I have labeled as the pandemic of the mind which affects the socioeconomic strata of a society.

Some may argue that "prophet" may not be the correct title for Reg. They would look at his life's work and say that the natural conclusions of his experiences were inevitable. I strongly disagree. Those with sight do not always see, those with minds do not always reason, and those with hearts do not always feel; particularly for anyone other than themselves or in their own self-interest. Reg channeled all three of those attributes, and added a soul that loves his fellow man, especially the underdog. He fully embraced his surroundings in his formative years and from that decided how he would live his life. He did not succumb to racial injustice and disparate treatment but chose to walk with dignity, intellect, and a composed view of his own self-worth. That is how this Black man walked down the streets of Jackson, Mississippi in the early 1960s registering other Black people to vote. Or was able to walk down the streets of Johannesburg, South Africa in the 1970's with his White wife and go to a dance in a fancy hotel. Then later walk down those same streets with her and their mixed-race children amid the specter of apartheid. All while in the face of mortal peril, all leaning on his belief in self and the mission that his Creator had for him.

Reg learned to clearly see this pandemic through the experiences in his life, both at home and abroad. I believe it is even more visible to those who are on the offending side of the mentality, though others also view yet turn a blind eye to it, using convention to make excuses for their privilege. History has shown such examples as White slave owners who perversely used the Holy Bible passages to endorse their superiority over the captives and to embolden their chicanery. What Reg was able to witness first-hand was that this mental disease was not just pervasive in the Illinois cities of East St. Louis, Champaign, or Carbondale, or even in the states of Mississippi, Alabama, or Kentucky, but could also be found in the African countries of Upper Volta, Kenya, Swaziland, South Africa, etc., extending even farther to the other five continents.

What White America was doing pre- and post-slavery was synonymous with apartheid in South Africa, anti-Semite atrocities in Nazi Germany, the colonization of Aboriginals in Australia or Black Africans by Europeans on the African continent, to name a few. Even more current the ethnic cleansing efforts in Bosnia and Afghanistan highlight the sustaining quality of this mind pandemic.

Reg always says to me how important it is to know history lest you are doomed to repeat it. He also is a huge proponent of learning more about the world that we live in; for it is there that you will see the differences in people and understand the commonality of our life situations. My father also taught me that. Reg encourages all to travel, learn a new language, and listen to the people before trying to "fix" their issues with your convention. This is inoculation or remedy to our mental pandemic, and how we communicate and support one another as we move towards a cure.

I can hear the shouts of SOCIALISM coming through the air. In any great society, there is a compromise of democracy and socialism, for neither alone is completely right nor completely wrong. The definitions of both have been skewed over the centuries by those suffering from the socioeconomic pandemic and used to meet their capitalistic ideals. Some people are raised in a society with generational suppressive socioeconomic mores, like young Afrikaners during the height of apartheid in South

Africa. With no external catalyst to highlight the flaws in their thinking, they are left with only their moral fortitude in humanity to change their ways. Reg embodies the moral fortitude that can break the cycle of these generational mores. He challenged the system in Cape Town and Johannesburg during the 1970s with his work and his family by showing an alternate view of life for the locals. It is also easily seen in Judith Katz's letter to Reg and Edna upon her attendance at their wedding referenced earlier in section "Three Score – from Swaziland to Swaggerland". His overall life's work has been a challenge to unnatural systemic norms both at home and abroad.

Reg's life has created a path for us to be the moral fortitude this world needs. He has set us on a quest to be the cure to the socioeconomic pandemic. So, discriminate what you allow to enter your mind, filter the thoughts that you allow in, and purge the impurities that slip by, always remembering that the Creator made us each unique and endowed us with specific gifts. And like a puzzle comprised of many colors and shapes, when all pieces are included, our senses behold the splendor of our creation, the beautiful tapestry of life. We may only see glimpses of it in our lifetimes, but our life's works should be dedicated to completing the puzzle, no matter how daunting or dangerous it may seem, for this, Reg, and I both believe, may be the answer to the age-old question of why we were created. Go forth and excise those socioeconomic Guinea worms of modern minds! The world is waiting on you with bated breath… Thank you, Reginald Edwin Petty, for your service to mankind.

# ABOUT THE AUTHOR

Jaye P. Willis is a product of a parochial school education in East St. Louis, Illinois, from the late 1960's to the early 1980's. She is a graduate of Southern Illinois University in Carbondale, Illinois, with a Bachelor of Science degree in Advanced Technical Studies (commonly known as Information Systems Management). She is also a certified Information Technology Project Manager, having earned Associates and Masters Certificates from George Washington University in Washington, DC. Jaye was employed with the United States Department of the Treasury for over 30 years, the last half as a Senior Project Manager, before retiring in 2019.

To create a level of balance in her life, Jaye joined the Eugene B. Redmond Writer's Club in East St. Louis, Illinois, in 2007. Since then, she has progressed into a published poet, sought after spoken word artist, and a published author. She has performed her works in St. Louis, Missouri, Atlanta, Georgia, New York, New York and Little Rock, Arkansas. She is also a motivational speaker on personal to professional topics and has made presentations in Buffalo, New York, Nashville, Tennessee, Corpus Christi, Texas, Portland, Oregon, Milwaukee, Wisconsin and at her alma mater in Carbondale, Illinois.

Jaye was raised in a household where books were always present. She gorged herself on such works as The Biography of Patrice Lumumba,

Mein Kampf, The Philosophies and Opinions of Marcus Garvey, and various books on Paul Robeson, Shirley Chisolm, George Washington and Thomas Jefferson, the Encyclopedia Britannica, the Oxford English Dictionary and Roget's Thesaurus. Her parents wanted her to have a broad education, encompassing various viewpoints, so that she would always maintain an open mind. The prevailing thought was if you want to understand a person or thing, you must study it, even if you do not embrace the beliefs.

It is with this open mind, expanse of knowledge and her life experiences that she presents this unique format of a praise song biography, including encapsulating Mr. Petty's experiences in scores (20-year periods), sprinkling in Black history facts, and introducing and ending each score with an original poetic piece from her and him, respectively.

# INDEX

## A

ACTION 36
Adams, Valarie 103
African Development Corporation (ADC) 33
African Development Foundation (ADF) 64
African Family Film Foundation 90
African National Congress (ANC) 77
Alpha Kappa Alpha Sorority, Incorporated 16
Aluminum Ore Company 9
American Revolution 11
AmeriCorps 36
Amos and Andy 15
Apartheid 63, 105, 115, 116
Attucks, Crispus x, 11

## B

Baraka, Amiri 36
Belleville News Democrat Newspaper 90, 94
Belt, Christopher, Illinois State Senator 95
Black Arts Movement 36
Black Lives Matter Movement xi
Boston Massacre 11
Botswana 38, 75
Breckenridge, Kentucky x

Brown, Joseph A., SJ; Ph.D. 1, 3, 72, 73, 99, 104
Burkina Faso x
Bush, Gordon, Mayor 77, 95

## C

Cahokia Mounds State Historic Site 10
Cambridge, Godfrey 36
Campbell, GiGi 103
Cannon, Mary 100
Carmichael, Stokely x, 34, 35, 108
Carter, Jimmy, U.S. President x, 62
Charlotte Amalie, Virgin Islands 37
Checker, Chubby 104
Chicago, Illinois 92, 104
Chisolm, Shirley, U.S. Congresswoman 29, 120
Christian Activity Center 107
Clayborne, James, Illinois State Senator 95
Clements, Kevin 73, 75, 104
Clifford, Sandy 73
Collins, Hank 61, 62
Costello, Jerry, Illinois State Representative 95
Country Director 61, 62, 104
Crenshaw, Roscoe 98
Currie, Willie 13, 100

## D

Datcher, Michael 98
Davis, Angela 35
Davis, Miles 36, 37, 92, 102
Dawson, Dr. Carrie 95
Denmark 92, 93
Devlin, Robert 73
Dorsey, Daphne 103
DuBois, W.E.B. 99
Durban, South Africa 77
Durbin, Richard 'Dick', U.S. Senator 95

## E

East Saint Louis, Illinois 7, 76
East Saint Louis Race Riots 99
East St. Louis 1917 Centennial Commission and Cultural Initiative (CCCI) 99
East St. Louis 1917 Centennial Commission Cultural Initiative (EStL 1917 99
East St. Louis Higher Education Building 100
East St. Louis Monitor Newspaper 91
East St. Louis Renaissance Literary Arts Press 90
East St. Louis Senior High School 12, 102
Edmund Pettus Bridge 34, 108
Educational Resources International (ERI), Incorporated 73
Edwards, Dr. Harry xi, 100, 109
Egypt 75
Enterprise Community Vision 20/20 group 90
Eugene B. Redmond Writers Club 119
Eugene Haynes Collection 93
Executive Director 83, 90
Executive Director Taale Leafi Rosellini 90

## F

Fairview Heights, Illinois 76
Federal Bureau of Investigation 29
Ferraro, Geraldine, U.S. Vice-Presidential Candidate 95
Ford, Gerald, U.S. President x, 62
Ford, Vann E. 90
Fox, Tom 100
Franklin, Stanley 108
Freeman, Roland L. 79

## G

Gandi, Mahatma 64
Garvey, Marcus 120
General Accounting Office (GAO) 64
General Learning Corporation (GLC) 35
George Washington University 119
Ghana 37, 75, 104
Grand Marais State Park 10
Granger, Rev. Kendall 108
Greenwood, LaToya, Illinois State Representative 95
Gregory, Dick 13, 15, 28
Guinea worms v, xii, 109, 117

## H

Haley, Johnetta 84
Harlem, New York 11, 36, 37
Harris, Jerome iii
Harris, Kevin 103
Haynes, Eugene 92, 93
Hicks, John H. 63
Hilliard, Constance 64
Historically Black Colleges and Universities (HBCU) 14
Hoffman, Jay. Illinois State Representative 95
Hooks, Sr., Robert 36
Hoover, J. Edgar 29
Humboldt State University 61

## I
Illinois State University, Bloomington, Illinois 9

## J
Jack Benny Show 15
Jackson, Mississippi 115
Jackson, Rev. Jesse 34, 61, 94
Jefferson, Thomas, U.S. President 120
Jennings, Emani 103
Job Corps x, 28
Johannesburg, South Africa 115
Johns Hopkins University 73
Johnson, Lyndon B., U.S. President x, 62
Jones, LeRoi 36
Julliard School in New York 92

## K
Kappa Alpha Psi Fraternity, Incorporated 14
Katherine Dunham 83, 102
Katherine Dunham Centers for Arts and Humanities (KDCAH) 83
Katz, Judith 80, 101, 117
Kennedy, John F., U.S. President x, 29, 62, 66
Kenya 37, 56, 58, 61, 62, 63, 75, 105, 116
Kern, Mark, St. Clair County Board Chairman 95
King, Jr., Dr. Martin Luther x, 34, 108
Klaus, Lucy 28
Krause, Richard \"R.J.\" 84

## L
Latimer, Anne 104
Latimer, Halima 105
Lawson, Linda 91
Lee, Sylvester 'Sunshine' 108
Lee, Tiffany Grimmett 108
Lessie Bates Neighborhood House 76, 78

Levine, David 38, 63, 80, 100, 101
Lewis, John, U.S. Congressman x, 34, 108
Liberia 63
Lincoln Senior High School in East St. Louis, Illinois 12
Lincoln University at Jefferson City, Missouri 14, 92, 93
Lumpkin, Charlois 103
Lythcott, George I. 37
Lythcott, Michael 36

## M
Mahoney, Dr. Carolyn 93
Mali 75
Mandela, Nelson x, 77
Margolis, Fred 38
Martin, Eugene 73
Mauritania 104, 105
McHenry, Donald, U.S. Ambassador xi, 100, 109
McKinney, Percy, St. Clair County Assessor 95
Metro East Church-Based Citizens' Organization (M.E.C.C.O.) 83
Mondale, Walter, U.S. Presidential Candidate 94, 95
Mozambique 70, 105

## N
National Association for the Advancement of Colored People (NAACP) 77
National Endowment for the Arts 90
National Institute of Health (NIH) 37
National Museum of African American History and Culture 34
Native American 11, 60
Navajo Indian 60
Neely, Beatrice Hunter 95
Negro 7, 10, 11, 13, 91, 92
Nigeria 105

Nkrumah, President Kwame 37
Northwestern University 62

## O
Oberlin College, Oberlin, Ohio 36
Office of Economic Opportunity (OEO) 36
Orr, Attorney Louis x

## P
Pandemic v, xi, 82, 106, 108, 115, 116, 117
Paradise, Curtis Louise 100
Paris, France 92
Parks, Jr., Alvin, Mayor 95, 99
Payne, Shirley 104
Peabody, Bessie 16
Permetti, Joseph 75
Petty, Amina 56, 57, 58, 59, 60, 61, 79, 100, 101
Petty, Anthony Tony 33
Petty, Edna Patterson iii, 60, 78, 79, 80, 81, 82, 83, 90, 91, 93, 94, 95, 99, 104, 117
Petty, Elijah 60
Petty, Helen 2, 7, 9, 60, 95
Petty, Joel 56, 58, 59, 60, 100, 101
Petty, Jr., Bruce Anthony 8
Petty, Lucy 28, 34, 58, 63, 73, 75, 79
Pfeifer, Sandra 90
Plessy vs. Ferguson 11
P&P Enterprises 94
Puerto Rico 36, 38, 75

## R
Racism v, 13, 15, 65, 66, 81, 106, 109, 115
Rafferty, Daniel 35
Redmond, Dr. Eugene 36, 103, 119
Rice, Jimmy 103
Richardson, Ann 73

Robeson, Paul 120
Rochester, Eddie 15

## S
Saint Louis Gateway Arch ix
Saint Louis, Missouri 7, 8
Saint Louis University 72
Saudi Arabia 75
Savage, Charmaine 100, 103
Savage, Lorenzo 100
Savage, Theodore Ted 13
Scott, Dred 8
Scott, Johnny 77
Secretary General Alfred Nzo 77
segregation 11, 92
Segregation 13
Selma, Alabama 34, 108
Seychelles 62, 63, 105
Shannon, Dr. William 35
Shannon, Tasha 103
Shawnee, Oklahoma 37
Shipp, Paulette 103
Shriver, Jr., Sargent 29
South Africa 57, 63, 78, 105, 116, 117
South African President Nelson Mandela 77
Southern Illinois University at Carbondale, Illinois 2, 15, 73, 119
Southern Illinois University at Edwardsville, Illinois 84, 90
St. Louis Cardinals 13
St. Louis Community College 100
St. Louis Post Dispatch Newspaper 63
Suber, Edna and Fay 91
Swaziland 38, 56, 57, 58, 62, 63, 75, 94, 104, 105, 116, 117

## T
Teer, Barbara Ann 36
Theising, Dr. Andrew 90

Third World  68, 71, 72
Tutu, Bishop Desmond  77

## U
University of Illinois at Champaign/Urbana  14, 35
University of Pennsylvania  64
Upper Volta  35, 116
U.S. Agency for International Development (USIAD)  64
U.S. Agency on International Development (USIAD)  75
U.S. Department of the Treasury  119
U.S. Information Agency  63
U.S. Peace Corps  29, 36, 38, 65
U.S. State Department  39
US Virgin Islands  36, 37

## V
volunteers  38, 62, 67, 68, 75, 104, 105
Volunteers in Service to America (VISTA)  36

## W
Washington, DC  9, 34, 35, 36, 58, 63, 75, 80, 82, 100, 119
Washington, George, U.S. President  119, 120
Washington University of St. Louis, Missouri  94
Weathers, Dr. Henry  x
Webster University in St. Louis, Missouri  107
Wells Barnett, Ida B.  91, 99
Wharton, Judge Milton  103
Willis, Jaye P.  1, 101, 119
Willis, Jered R.  101
Willis, Quintin  103
World Bank  64, 104

## X
X, Malcolm  x

## Y
Yale University  73
YMCA of Greater St. Louis, Missouri  84, 94
Younge, Wyvetter, Illinois House of Representatives  77
Young, Lawanda  103

## Z
Zimbabwe  105

Printed in the USA
CPSIA information can be obtained
at www.ICGtesting.com
LVHW072100300824
789726LV00008B/120